Action UK! 2

Begleitheft zu den Filmsequenzen

von Frank Haß, Dr. Werner Kieweg, Harald Weisshaar, Axel Plitsch und Nicole Richter

Ernst Klett Verlag
Stuttgart · Leipzig

Inhaltsverzeichnis

Vorwort 3

Unit 1
Unterrichtsvorschläge
- A. Focus on: Back to school 6
- B. That's life: BMXing 8

Worksheets
- A. Focus on: Back to school 10
- B. That's life: BMXing 12

Unit 2
Unterrichtsvorschläge
- A. Focus on: The weekend 14
- B. That's life: The London Eye 16

Worksheets
- A. Focus on: The weekend 18
- B. That's life: The London Eye 20

Unit 3
Unterrichtsvorschläge
- A. Focus on: Fashion 22
- B. That's life: Friends? 24

Worksheets
- A. Focus on: Fashion 26
- B. That's life: Friends? 28

Unit 4
Unterrichtsvorschläge
- A. Focus on: Music 30
- B. That's life: Star Reporters 32

Worksheets
- A. Focus on: Music 34
- B. That's life: Star Reporters 36

Unit 5
Unterrichtsvorschläge
- A. Focus on: Healthy food 38
- B. That's life: Fit – fitter – the fittest 40

Worksheets
- A. Focus on: Healthy food 42
- B. That's life: Fit – fitter – the fittest 44

Unit 6
Unterrichtsvorschläge
- A. Focus on: Broughton Castle 46
- B. That's life: A trip to the seaside 48

Worksheets
- A. Focus on: Broughton Castle 50
- B. That's life: A trip to the seaside 52

Unit 7
Unterrichtsvorschläge
- A. Focus on: Typically British 54

Worksheets
- A. Focus on: Typically British 58

Lernportfolio 62

Glossar 63

Filmskripte 67

---

1. Auflage   1 ⁶ 5 4 3 2 | 2011 2010 2009 2008

Alle Drucke dieser Auflage sind unverändert und können im Unterricht nebeneinander verwendet werden.
Die letzte Zahl bezeichnet das Jahr des Druckes.

Das Werk und seine Teile sind urheberrechtlich geschützt. Jede Nutzung in anderen als den gesetzlich zugelassenen Fällen bedarf der vorherigen schriftlichen Einwilligung des Verlages. Hinweis zu § 52 a UrhG: Weder das Werk noch seine Teile dürfen ohne eine solche Einwilligung eingescannt und in ein Netzwerk eingestellt werden. Dies gilt auch für Intranets von Schulen und sonstigen Bildungseinrichtungen. Fotomechanische oder andere Wiedergabeverfahren nur mit Genehmigung des Verlages.

© Ernst Klett Verlag GmbH, Stuttgart 2007.
Alle Rechte vorbehalten.
Internetadresse: www.klett.de

Herausgeber: Frank Haß, Kirchberg; Dr. Werner Kieweg, Schwabmünchen; Harald Weisshaar, Bisingen
Autoren: Axel Plitsch, Wülfrath; Nicole Richter, Stuttgart
Unter Mitarbeit von: Annegret Preker-Franke, Bielefeld; Tanja Wiedmann, Lauffen
Redaktion: Birgit Piefke-Wagner (Außenredaktion), Joanne Popp

Layoutkonzeption: Wiebke Hengst, Ostfildern
Zeichnungen / Illustrationen: Martin Hoffmann, Stuttgart; Jaroslaw Schwarzstein, Hannover
Fotos: Gillian Bathmaker, Ernst Klett Verlag, Stuttgart; Master Kitchen, Ludwigsburg
Umschlaggestaltung: Koma Amok, Stuttgart; Ira Häußler

Satz: Meyle + Müller, Medien-Management, Pforzheim
Reproduktion: Meyle + Müller, Medien-Management, Pforzheim
Druck: Gulde-Druck GmbH, Tübingen

Printed in Germany
ISBN 978-3-12-585162-7

Vorwort

Liebe Kolleginnen und Kollegen,

viele von Ihnen haben durch die Arbeit mit *Action UK! 1* bereits die Vorzüge audiovisueller Unterrichtsmedien kennen gelernt. Nun liegt mit *Action UK! 2* dessen Fortsetzung vor. Der bewährten Konzeption des ersten Teils folgend, bietet *Action UK! 2* wieder sieben Episoden eines Jugendmagazins, die thematisch auf die Schülerbuchunits abgestimmt sind und den Rahmen für je zwei Filmsequenzen pro Unit bilden. In *Focus on* präsentieren die drei aus *Action UK! 1* bekannten Schülerreporter Maya, Josh und Greg wieder unterschiedliche Aspekte ihres Schullebens und ihrer Freizeit, und *That's life* zeigt kurze Spielszenen aus dem Alltag der britischen S. Die Episoden bauen nicht aufeinander auf, es können daher problemlos einzelne Episoden oder auch Sequenzen weggelassen werden. Wie in Teil 1 bietet *Try it out!* am Ende jeder Episode die Möglichkeit, einige Redemittel unterstützt durch die Schriftsprache eingehend zu betrachten.

Mögliche *Try it out! activities* sind

- *gap filling* (S bekommen den *Try it out!*-Teil als Lückentext und ergänzen die fehlenden Wörter aus dem Gedächtnis. Zur Überprüfung wird der Teil erneut gezeigt.)
- Mitsprechen und nach mehrmaligem Ansehen lautes Vorsprechen ohne Sprechvorbild (Ton ausstellen)
- Nach mehrmaligem Ansehen wird nur die Antwort vorgegeben, S sollen die Frage stellen.
- Rekonstruktion der Aussagen aus dem Gedächtnis (mögliche Hilfestellungen: schreiben Sie die Namen der Sprecher an die Tafel oder nennen Sie Satzanfänge.)
- Mündliches Ergänzen (S sehen den Dialog, beim zweiten Ansehen lesen und hören sie ihn auch. Lesen Sie ihn danach nochmals vor und ersetzen Sie dabei einen Satzteil bzw. ein Wort mit „mh-mhmh". S erraten den weggelassenen Satzteil und ergänzen ihn im Satz.)

Projektarbeit mit Action UK!

Zusätzlich zum Einsatz des Films am Ende jeder Schülerbuchunit und seiner Aufbereitung anhand von *pre-viewing*, *while-viewing* und *post-viewing activities* ist *Action UK!* auch sehr gut als Vorbild für ein eigenes Filmprojekt Ihrer Klasse geeignet. Im Folgenden ein Vorschlag für den Aufbau eines solchen Projekts:

School moviemakers

What about making a video about your own school? Then you could

- put on a video show at your next school party
- send it to your partner school in Britain, the USA or elsewhere in the world, or
- give a copy of it to all who leave the school

Preparations: a plan and a storyboard

First of all, make a plan. Discuss what could be interesting to other people. Then decide who is going to do what. You can work in two or three groups. You also need a storyboard for your film. Write and/or draw all the information you want to give in frames on a sheet of paper. Add the people you are going to talk to and the places you are going to show. Decide how you are going to structure the video (beginning, middle and end) and how you can present the material.

Possible scenes of the video

1. You can start with a short description of the school's past. You should think of the following points:
   - Who or where can you get information from?
   - How can you make your description more lively (background, reading text or speaking freely, clothes, etc.)?

2. Then it would be nice to show the school as it is today. You can
   - give facts and figures
   - show the different subjects
   - interview teachers
   - describe classrooms and other parts of your school
   - ask pupils for their opinions on subjects, teachers, the school, etc.

3. You can show everyday school life.
   - Describe a normal day at school.
   - Spend a whole day with one pupil and film what he/she does. But don't forget to ask permission (pupils and teachers) before you start. You can do the same with another pupil who is older/younger.

4. Show how pupils get to school every day.
   - Find out where they come from (village, town).

- How many kilometres/metres do they have to travel/walk to school?
- How long does it take them to get to school?

5. Film what pupils do in breaks.
- Do this with different classes in the short and longer breaks.
- What do the girls do? What do the boys do? What do they do together?

6. What happens in the afternoons at school?
- Find out who stays at school after lessons (pupils, teachers, others).
- What do they do (school work, repair work, cleaning, clubs, sports, etc.)?
- Interview the people who are there in the afternoon.

7. Former pupils
- Do you know any former pupils of your school who have become famous, e.g. sportsmen/sportswomen, actors, politicians, people with unusual hobbies, etc.?
- Find out about them and interview them about their time at your school.

8. Give a summary of what you think about your school.
- What is good about it? What is not so good?
- Maybe you can suggest what could be changed at your school.

The final version

When you have done all this – or some of these things – look through all the material you have filmed, discuss it and decide what should be used and what shouldn't. Then you can edit the material and put together the final version.
Now you need a good title. Brainstorming in a group can be a good idea to find an interesting title that makes people curious. *Our school sounds boring*, but what about *Goethe goes to Hollywood*? Don't forget to add some background music, maybe different kinds of music for different parts of the video. And sound effects would be nice, too! Think about what you can do with your hands, a piece of paper or instruments.
Just two more things: a video shouldn't be too long or it becomes boring. And it should be fun. So have fun making your school movie!

10 Golden Rules

Abschließend noch einige allgemeine Tipps zur Arbeit mit *Action UK!*:

1. Nehmen Sie sich nicht zu viel auf einmal vor. Beginnen Sie langsam mit bescheidenen Arbeitsaufträgen. Weniger ist oft mehr. Auch wenn die S sich den Film anfänglich nur ansehen um zu erkennen, wie viel sie eigentlich schon auf Englisch verstehen können, ist das die Mühe wert.
2. Machen Sie den S klar, dass es sich nicht um einen aktionsgeladenen Kinofilm handelt, sondern um kleine Episoden, die dem Lernen und der Vorbereitung des Sehens von längeren Filmen dienen.
3. Beziehen Sie die S in die Planung und Durchführung der Unterrichtssequenzen mit ein. Dies motiviert und fördert das autonome Lernen.
4. Finden Sie das richtige Maß an Erklärungen. Zu viel macht das Zuschauen langweilig, zu wenig überfordert die S und sie verlieren das Interesse.
5. Beschränken Sie besonders die Aufgaben während des Hörens/Sehens auf ein schaffbares Maß.
6. Geben Sie Beispiele, damit die S die Aufgaben besser verstehen.
7. Unterbrechen Sie die Sequenzen während des Ansehens nicht zu oft. Scheuen Sie sich aber auch nicht, Sequenzen mehrmals abzuspielen.
8. Lassen Sie keinen methodischen Schematismus aufkommen, dieser produziert Langeweile. Variieren Sie die Übungen. Nutzen Sie den Film nicht für rein grammatikalisch/lexikalisch orientierte Übungsabläufe. Das Begleitheft zu den Filmsequenzen gibt Ihnen vielfältige Anregungen.
9. Ganz besonders wichtig: Probieren Sie alles (besonders das einwandfreie Funktionieren der Technik) vorher aus.
10. Leihen Sie den Film auch an S aus, so dass diese ihn sich mehrmals zu Hause ansehen können.

Viewing skills

Ziel von *Action UK!* ist es auch, die S in zunehmendem Maße zu autonomem Arbeiten mit Hör-Sehtexten anzuleiten. Folgende Strategien sollten sie selbstständig anwenden können, wenn nicht durch die Lehrkraft ein anderes Vorgehen vorgeschrieben ist:

Step 1: Prepare yourself
Stimme dich selbst auf das Ansehen der Filmsequenz ein. Welche Erwartungen hast du? Was könnte der Inhalt/das Thema der Filmsequenz sein? Sammle Wörter und Wendungen, die dir beim Verstehen helfen könnten.

Step 2: Watch for gist
Schaue dir die Filmsequenz zunächst einmal an und versuche zu erfassen, worum es geht. Waren deine Vermutungen richtig? Kümmere dich nicht um Wendungen oder Einzelwörter, die du vielleicht noch nicht verstanden hast.

Step 3: Watch for details
Sieh dir die Filmsequenz ein zweites Mal an. Nun mach dir Notizen zum Inhalt. Schreibe auf:
– wer im Film vorkommt
– wo etwas geschieht
– wann etwas geschieht
– was geschieht
– warum das geschieht
– welche Folgen das hat

Step 4: Give your opinion
Fasse die gesehene Sequenz mit eigenen Worten zusammen und sage deine Meinung zur gesehenen Episode.

Step 5: Evaluate
Überlege, inwieweit dir die gesehene Episode beim Lernen und besseren Verstehen geholfen hat. Was sonst würde dir beim Lernen helfen? Sprich mit deinem Lehrer darüber.

Aufbau und Einsatz des Begleitheftes

Vorliegendes Begleitheft bietet Ihnen vielfältige Unterrichtsanregungen und Kopiervorlagen zu *Action UK! 2*. Die Hinweise für den Unterricht und die Worksheets sind innerhalb der Episoden den Sequenzen *A. Focus on* und *B. That's life* zugeordnet. Wie in Band 1 sind die folgenden Materialien in *pre-viewing*, *while-viewing* und *post-viewing activities* unterteilt. Innerhalb dieser Phasen finden Sie sinnvoll aufeinander aufbauende Unterrichtsschritte, die zumeist den Einsatz der *Worksheets* beinhalten. Die Angabe sämtlicher Lösungen, praktische Tipps und konkrete Track- bzw. Minutenangaben erleichtern Ihnen dabei die Arbeit. Des Weiteren finden Sie in den Unterrichtshinweisen eine tabellarische Zusammenfassung der *storyline*, eine Übersicht über die sprachlichen und kommunikativen Ziele sowie Angaben zum neuen Wortschatz der jeweiligen Sequenz. Wichtig in der Arbeit mit dem Film ist, dass die S lernen mit unbekanntem Wortschatz umzugehen, d. h. es soll nur der sinntragende Wortschatz vorentlastet werden. Im Anhang finden Sie ein Lernportfolio, ein Glossar mit dem gesamten unbekannten Wortschatz sowie die kompletten Filmskripte.

Nun wünschen wir Ihnen viel Erfolg und Freude bei der Arbeit mit *Action UK!*.

Frank Haß

Unit 1
A. Focus on: Back to school

Overview

Sequence	Track	Duration	Characters	Storyline
Studio	Track 1	00:55	Dave, Rani	
A. Focus on: Back to school	Track 2	08:09	Maya, Josh, Greg, teacher	Josh, Greg and Maya do a tour around Thomas Tallis School on their first day after the summer holidays.

Ziele
- S lernen den Ablauf des Schultages an einer englischen Schule kennen
- Festigung des *simple present:* über etwas sprechen, das regelmäßig geschieht

Neuer Wortschatz

series, studio, reporter, to take a look, crazy, report, soon, until, in front of, camera, star, to joke, over to you, same, as, Miss, to make sure, Registration, to call out, to check, playing field, PE kit, notebook, Action!, to read out, camping, to sound, What else happened?, ketchup, Australia, rugby, Cut!

Pre-viewing

Reporters want to know everything

Worksheet, p. 10

In dieser Aufgabe begegnen S den Reportern Josh, Maya und Greg (auf der Leinwand) und Dave und Rani (im Studio) wieder. Die Aufgabe, in der S mit Hilfe der Fragen Aussagen über ihre eigene Schule machen, führt in die Thematik Schultag an einer englischen Schule ein und bereitet so auf die Videosequenz vor.
Lernstärkere S fassen die Aussagen zu einem Text zusammen, für den die Fragen das Gerüst bilden. In lernschwächeren Gruppen geben Sie Satzanfänge vor (vgl. Lösungsvorschlag), die S beenden.

TIPP
Das Foto auf der Kopiervorlage hilft auch denjenigen S, die bisher noch nicht mit *Action UK!* gearbeitet haben, sich rasch in der folgenden ersten Sequenz des Films zurechtzufinden. Die Nummerierung entspricht den Fragen 1 bis 5, sodass sich S rasch ein Bild von den Personen machen können.

Lösungsvorschlag
1. The name of my school is Velbert-Langenberg-Gymnasium.
2. There are about 650 pupils at our school. 3. No, I'm not. I'm in Year 7.
4. There are 31 pupils in my class, 15 boys and 16 girls.
5. Lessons start at 8.00 and finish at 13.20.
   But on Wednesdays and Thursdays they finish at 14.15.
6. My favourite subject is PE. 7. There are a lot of clubs at our school.
8. We don't get lunch at school, so the kids eat their sandwiches in the breaks.
9. My best friends at school are Marten, Tobi and Samia.
10. There is no school uniform at our school.

Mögliche Lösung für eine Textproduktion
My school is called Velbert-Langenberg-Gymnasium. Langenberg is a small town near Essen. There are about 650 pupils and about 40 teachers at our school. I am in Year 7, in class 7a, and there are 15 boys and 16 girls in my class. Usually school starts at 8 o'clock, but sometimes we start later. We finish at twenty past one, but on Wednesdays and Thursdays we finish at quarter past two. That's not so nice. My favourite subject is PE, because we often play football and our teacher is very nice. We have two PE lessons and one swimming lesson a week. There are a lot of clubs at our school. You can play football or learn to play the guitar or the keyboard.
We don't have a cafeteria at our school but a little shop where we can buy sandwiches, other snacks and drinks. My best friends are Marten, Tobi and Samia. We always play table tennis in the breaks. We don't have school uniforms. That's really good.

Unterrichtsvorschläge 1

While-viewing

A day at Thomas Tallis

Worksheet, p. 11

a) Zeigen Sie zuerst die kurze Studioszene und besprechen Sie dann mit S die Aufgabe der Kopiervorlage. Geben Sie S etwas Zeit alle Sätze einmal zu lesen und die Bilder zu betrachten. Spielen Sie nun die Filmsequenz vor. Im Anschluss daran werden die Lösungen vorgetragen. Ggf. wird ein Mustersatz an der Tafel vorgegeben: *"I've got this cool new bag with me!"* goes with picture 1.

b) S können zunächst ihre Antworten zu Teilaufgabe b) mit Bleistift eintragen. Spielen Sie den Film ein weiteres Mal vor, damit S ihre Antworten überprüfen und überarbeiten können. Vergleich der Lösungen im Plenum.

> **Lösung**
> a) picture 1 – c; picture 2 – d; picture 3 – h; picture 4 – g; picture 5 – b; picture 6 – a; picture 7 – e; picture 8 – f.
> b) 1. In front of the school; 2. At Registration; 3. In Assembly; 4. In the classroom; 5. In the playground; 6. In the school shop; 7. In the cafeteria; 8. After school

TIPP
In lernschwächeren Gruppen können Sie die Sequenz ein zweites Mal vorspielen. Dabei überprüfen S ihre Ergebnisse und korrigieren. In lernstärkeren Gruppen können die in dieser Aufgabe behandelten Szenen aus dem Film nachgestellt werden, wobei S auch weitere Sätze (auch solche, die sie aus dem Film behalten haben) verwenden.

Post-viewing

Josh's timetable

Worksheet, p. 11

Lassen Sie S die Aufgabe selbstständig lösen. Dabei verarbeiten S die Ergebnisse der vorhergehenden Aufgabe und vervollständigen Joshs Stundenplan für den ersten Schultag.

> **Lösung**
> | | | | |
> |---|---|---|---|
> | 8.40 – 8.50 | Registration/Assembly | 13.10 – 14.10 | Lunch break |
> | 8.50 – 10.50 | Lessons | 14.10 – 15.10 | Lesson |
> | 10.50 – 11.10 | Break | 15.10 – 15.20 | Afternoon tutorial |
> | 11.10 – 13.10 | Lessons | 15.20 – 16.30 | Samba Club |

TIPP
Bei der Ergebnisüberprüfung sagen S jeweils in einem oder mehreren Sätzen, was dort stattfindet. Beispiel: *The kids are in the cafeteria. Here the pupils can buy lunch.*

A school alphabet

In einer weiteren Phase sammeln S Wörter, die zum Wortfeld Schule gehören, und ordnen diese alphabetisch. Schreiben Sie das Alphabet und die Überschrift 'A school alphabet' an die Tafel und erklären Sie S, dass Adjektive, Nomen und Verben genannnt werden können. Geben Sie ggf. Beispielwörter vor, etwa:
 D = drama
 I = interesting
 K = kid
Weisen Sie S darauf hin, dass zwei Buchstaben (X und Z) nicht belegt werden können.

L *Let's make a school alphabet. Find school words for the letters of the alphabet you can see on the board. You can use nouns, verbs and adjectives. Watch out! There are no words for the letters X and Z.*

TIPP
Interessanter wird es, wenn Sie diese Aufgabe als Wettspiel durchführen lassen. S bekommen fünf bis acht Minuten Zeit, so viele Wörter wie möglich zu finden. Gewonnen hat, wer die meisten (richtig geschriebenen) Wörter findet.

> **Lösungsvorschläge**
> A = Assembly, Art, answer, to arrive, angry; B = boring, break, bag, book;
> C = cafeteria, club, classroom, class, cool, correct; D = dance, drama, difficult;
> E = English, eat, exercise book, end, education, easy, experiment; F = food, friend, French;
> G = German, Geography; H = History, holidays, homework, hate, hungry, help;
> I = interesting; J = to joke, jacket, juice; K = kit, kid, know; L = learn, lesson, lunchtime, leave; M = Maths, miss, music room, menu, meet; N = notebook, noun; O = open, order, organize; P = playground, planner, playing field, pencil, PE, pupil; Q = question, quiz, quiet; R = Registration, Religious Education; S = subject, school shop, Science, students, sandwich; T = teach, tutor group, teacher, timetable, trousers, Technology; U = uniform; V = visit, vocabulary, verb; W = workbook, worksheet, whisper; X = ?; Y = year; Z = ?

1 Unterrichtsvorschläge

B. That's life: BMXing

Overview

Sequence	Track	Duration	Characters	Storyline
Studio	Track 3	00:27	Dave, Rani	
B: That's life: BMXing	Track 4	04:59	Greg, Maya, Maya's sister Stacey	Maya meets Greg to have a go on his old BMX bike. While they are busy getting the old bike adjusted, Stacey 'steals' Greg's new bike and disappears. To make up for her misbehaviour, she has to buy ice-creams for Greg and Maya and to hand over the crisps she is eating to Greg.

Ziele
- einen Streich durchschauen und verbalisieren
- eine Geschichte nacherzählen
- einen Tagebucheintrag schreiben

Neuer Wortschatz
busy, BMX, helmet, glove, knee pad, dangerous, rucksack, low, Just a minute., poor, next time

Pre-viewing

Greg and his BMX bike

Worksheet, p. 12

Zeigen Sie die Studioszene und greifen Sie Daves erwartungsfrohen Kommentar "Well, I'd like to see Greg on his BMX – it sounds great fun." auf. S äußern sich spontan dazu, welche Rolle das Fahrradfahren in ihrer Freizeit spielt, welche Art von Fahrrad sie haben (bzw. gern hätten), was sie mit dem Rad unternehmen und welche Kleidung sie hierbei tragen. In dieser Phase kann zum Verständnis des Films benötigter Wortschatz eingeführt werden. Verteilen Sie dann den Lückentext, der auf Greg als eine der zentralen Figuren des Videos einstimmt und das Wortfeld „Fahrradfahren" erweitert und festigt. Dass S bei dieser Übung einige der Wörter noch nicht sicher beherrschen, ist hier beabsichtigt. S werden die Lösung durch das Ausschlussverfahren finden.

> **Lösung:**
> To go BMXing you need a <u>helmet</u>, <u>gloves</u> and <u>knee pads</u>. Sometimes I take a <u>rucksack</u> with me. There are <u>sandwiches</u> in it, because I'm always hungry. BMXing is easy, but it gets difficult if you try to do a <u>trick</u>. You must be very careful, because sometimes BMXing can be <u>dangerous</u>. Last year I joined the BMX <u>Club</u>. It's great fun, but sometimes my mum gets angry, because I come home so <u>dirty</u>. Then I have to <u>clean</u> my bike. But that's OK, because I love my BMX bike!

TIPP
Weisen Sie S darauf hin, den Text zunächst einmal ganz zu lesen und nur die Wörter einzusetzen, die sie sicher wissen. Die bereits benutzten Wörter aus der Box sollten von S durchgestrichen werden. Beim zweiten Lesen ergeben sich unbekanntere Wörter auch durch Assoziation: helmet = Helm oder knee pad = Knieschoner (knee ist S bekannt).

What's up after school today?

Worksheet, p. 12

Fordern Sie S auf, die Bilder aus dem Arbeitsblatt auszuschneiden und vor sich auf den Tisch zu legen. Weisen Sie S darauf hin, dass die Fotos nicht in der richtigen Reihenfolge abgedruckt sind. S diskutieren die mögliche Abfolge der in den Fotos dargestellten Filmszenen und äußern Vermutungen über das, was Maya, Greg und Stacey an diesem Nachmittag widerfahren ist. Sammeln Sie Ideen für eine denkbare *storyline* unkommentiert am OHP oder an der Tafel. Nach der *while-viewing*-Phase können Sie gemeinsam mit S überprüfen, welche Vermutungen über die in dieser Sequenz erzählte Geschichte zutreffend waren.

While-viewing

Find the right order

Erklären Sie, dass die Fotos nun in die Reihenfolge gebracht werden müssen, die die Filmgeschichte vorgibt. Zeigen Sie den Film einmal vollständig. S überprüfen und korrigieren ggf. die in der *pre-viewing*-Phase vorgenommene Anordnung ihrer Bilder. Zeigen Sie die Sequenz erneut und überprüfen Sie im Anschluss die Arbeit der S, bevor sie die Bilder in ihr Heft einkleben. S besprechen das im jeweiligen Foto dargestellte Geschehen mit einem Partner/einer Partnerin und formulieren passende Bildunterschriften. Überprüfen Sie die Ergebnisse, indem Sie herumgehen. Eine gemeinsame Ergebnissicherung kann mithilfe einer Folie im Plenum erfolgen. Leistungsstärkere S können die Geschichte anhand der Szenenfotos auch mündlich nacherzählen. Diese Aufgabe kann auch als schriftliche Hausaufgabe gestellt werden.

> **Lösung zu a) und Lösungsvorschlag zu b):**
> a) 3, 1, 2, 4
> b) 1. Please, show me a trick, Greg. 2. You need a helmet, Maya.
>   3. Greg prepares his bike for Maya. 4. Stacey does a trick.

Worksheet, p. 12

TIPP

Kopieren Sie für die abschließende Ergebnisüberprüfung die Fotos in der richtigen Reihenfolge so auf eine Folie, dass Sie unter jedes Foto mit einem permanenten Folienstift Schreiblinien einfügen können. Decken Sie bei der Besprechung ein Foto nach dem anderen auf. S schreiben gelungene Bildunterschriften unter die Fotos.

Post-viewing

Stacey's trick

Zeigen Sie das Video erneut und lassen Sie S besonders auf die Mimik und Gestik von Stacey und ihr Verhalten im Video achten. Da in dieser Sequenz zwei Geschichten parallel stattfinden, dient diese Übung dazu, die Nebenhandlung zu verdeutlichen. Zudem üben S hier, die Geschichte von Greg und Maya aus einer anderen Perspektive zu betrachten.

> **Lösungsvorschlag:**
> 1. Oh, it's so boring here. Why can't Maya play a game with me? She talks and talks and talks.
> 2. That's a cool bike! Let's see. Maybe I can do some tricks on it.
> 3. Oh, that Greg! He thinks he is really cool! Is that all he can do? I'm much better.
> 4. Ha! Crisps! Nice! But look at those two. Maya is so stupid. She can't ride that bike. It's too low. But I can ride Greg's new bike!
> 5. Look at them! They can't see me! This bike is fantastic! Here I go!
> 6. Yessss! I can do Greg's trick. It's easy! Now let's try another trick. Oh no! Maya! And she is shouting. Let's go back.
> 7. What's wrong? They don't understand. I'm good at BMXing! But OK. OK! It's better to say sorry!
> 8. It's not fair! Stupid big sister! I haven't got any money for my own ice-cream! I want to have fun, too!

Worksheet, p. 13

TIPP

Leistungsschwächere Gruppen erhalten Sätze zu den Bildern (vgl. Lösungsvorschlag) in gemischter Form. S ordnen diese Sätze den Bildern zu.

TIPP

Leistungsstarke Gruppen verfassen einen Tagebucheintrag aus Staceys Sicht schriftlich. Gut als Hausaufgabe geeignet.

Unit 1
A. Focus on: Back to school

Pre-viewing

Reporters want to know everything

Dave and Rani who are in the studio and the three reporters Greg, Josh and Maya have got some questions for you about your school. Write down your answers.

1. Greg: Hi, there! My name's Greg, and I'm at Thomas Tallis School. What's the name of your school?

   You: _The name of my school_

2. Maya: Hello! It's me, Maya. And here's my first question. How many pupils are there at your school?

   You: _____

3. Josh: I'm Josh, and I'm in Year 10. Are you in Year 10, too?

   You: _No, I'm not. I'm_

4. Rani: And I'm Rani. How many pupils are there in your class? How many boys and how many girls?

   You: _____

5. Dave: My name is Dave and I'm in the studio with Rani. And here is my question for you. When do lessons start and finish at your school?

   You: _____

6. Greg: What is your favourite subject?

   You: _____

7. Josh: I go to the Film Club. Are there clubs at your school, too?

   You: _____

8. Greg: I'm always hungry. So here is an important question. Do you have lunch at school?

   You: _____

9. Rani: Who are your best friends at school?

   You: _____

10. Maya: Is there a school uniform at your school?

    You: _____

Worksheet 1

While-viewing

A day at Thomas Tallis

a) *Match the photos with the sentences from the video. Write the letters a–h in the boxes.*

In front of the school

a) Maya: We can buy our uniform and PE kit here, and pencils and notebooks, too.

b) Greg: Or have a snack.

c) Greg: I've got this cool new bag with me!

d) Maya: The teacher calls out all the names to check who is at school.

e) Josh: At lunchtime we can buy food and eat it in the cafeteria.

f) Josh: That's the end of a very busy day. It's 4.30 and we're going home.

g) Maya: We have lessons from 8.50 to 10.50.

h) Greg: Sometimes we go to Assembly in the hall.

b) *Watch and listen again. Where are the kids? Find titles for the photos and write them down.*

Post-viewing

Josh's timetable

Finish Josh's timetable for his first day at Thomas Tallis School after the summer holidays.

– 8.50		13.10 – 14.10	
–	Lessons	14.10 – 15.10	
–		15.10 – 15.20	Afternoon tutorial
– 13.10		15.20 –	

1 Worksheet

B. That's life: BMXing

Pre-viewing

Greg and his BMX bike

What does Greg tell Maya about his bike? Find the right words in the box and write them down.

knee pads   trick   dangerous   helmet   sandwiches   dirty   gloves   clean   rucksack   Club

To go BMXing you need a _____, _____ and

_____.

Sometimes I take a _____ with me. There are _____

in it, because I'm always hungry.

BMXing is easy, but it gets difficult if you try to do a _____.

You must be very careful, because sometimes BMXing can be _____.

Last year I joined the BMX _____.

It's great fun, but sometimes my mum gets angry, because I come home so _____.

Then I have to _____ my bike. But that's OK, because I love my BMX bike!

What's up after school today?

The pictures below are part of the story about an exciting afternoon in Greenwich. But they are not in the right order. Work with a partner. Cut the pictures out and put them in a good order.
*Discuss what is happening in **your** story.*

1

2

3

4

While-viewing

Find the right order

a) *Now watch the film and see if your idea for the story is right. Glue the pictures in the right order.*

b) *Find a good sentence for each picture.*

Worksheet 1

Post-viewing

Stacey's trick

What does Stacey think in each picture? Write down one or two sentences.

1. _____
2. _____
3. _____
4. _____
5. _____
6. _____
7. _____
8. _____

2 Unterrichtsvorschläge

Unit 2
A. Focus on: The weekend

Overview				
Sequence	Track	Duration	Characters	Storyline
Studio	Track 7	01:11	Dave, Rani	
A. Focus on: The weekend	Track 8	05:47	Maya, Josh, Greg, three boys and five girls	Maya, Josh and Greg interview pupils at Thomas Tallis School about what they did at the weekend. Then the reporters show three short films about their own weekend: Greg bought a song book and played his new guitar, Maya had a sleepover at her house and Josh filmed some places for his new film about London.

Ziele
- sich über das vergangene Wochenende unterhalten
- Festigung von Fragen und Antworten im *simple past*

Neuer Wortschatz

gardening, fishing, Let's get on with it., mine, around about, to go shopping, pocket money, cheapest, cameraman, surprised, string, a long time, to string, pretty, air, sometime, anytime, sleepover, hair, popstar, sleep, Like what?, to have a look, to get up to, all round, to film, Serpentine Lake, Buckingham Palace, queen, Trafalgar Square, Nelson's Column, Tower Bridge, Houses of Parliament, Gosh!, see you

Pre-viewing

Classroom survey: What did you do last weekend?

Bringen Sie als Requisite ein Mikrofon mit in den Englischunterricht. Mimen Sie einen Reporter und befragen Sie einzelne S, wie sie ihr letztes Wochenende einschätzen würden. Flüstern Sie, falls die unregelmäßigen Verbformen nicht korrekt wiedergegeben werden, ein. Schreiben Sie die Antworten in Kurzform an die Tafel.

Beispieldialog:
L: Paul, how was your weekend?
S: Cool, I played football with my friends.   TA: Cool
L: Did you stay at home or did you go out?
S: I went out on Saturday.   TA: went out on Saturday
L: David, what about you?
  Did you watch TV last weekend?
S: Yes, I did.
L: How much TV did you watch?
S: About 4 hours on Saturday.   TA: watched TV for 4 hours
L: Sarah, what did you do?
S: I visited my grandma on Sunday.   TA: visited her grandma

TIPP

Zur Vertiefung und Übung des *simple past* können S in ihr Heft schreiben, was sie über das Wochenende der befragten Mitschüler/innen wissen. Diese Aufgabe bietet sich auch als Hausaufgabe gut an.

Worksheet, p. 18

Verteilen Sie nun die Aufgabe 1 und lassen Sie S mindestens drei ihrer Mitschüler/innen auf diese Art und Weise interviewen und ihre Antworten in Stichworten notieren [Teilaufgabe a)]. Im Anschluss an die Interviews berichten möglichst viele S vor der Klasse über das Wochenende einer oder eines anderen S [Teilaufgabe b)].

Lösungsvorschlag zu b)
Laura's weekend was very nice. On Saturday she went to the park with her friends and played basketball. Her team won! On Sunday she stayed at home. She didn't watch TV, but she played computer games with her brother for four hours.

Teilaufgabe c): Um bei den S die Erwartungshaltung für die Videosequenz zu steigern, sollen sie sich nun in Einzelarbeit überlegen, wie britische Teenager ihrer Meinung nach ihr Wochenende verbringen. Das Wortfeld *weekend* kann dabei je nach Leistungsstand der Klasse in Form eines *brainstormings* oder einer strukturierten *mind map* (z. B. *places, people, activities*, etc.) erstellt werden.

> **Lösungen c)**
> *Individuelle Wortfelder*

TIPP
Die individuell strukturierten Wortfelder der S können später ergänzt werden, z. B. durch den Ideenaustausch untereinander oder durch die Erlebnisse der Charaktere im Video.

While-viewing

What did they do?

Stellen Sie die globale Frage *What do the pupils talk about?* und lassen Sie S während der Videosequenz dazu Stichworte notieren.
Lassen Sie S die Sequenz nun 1 x ansehen (nur die Interviews mit den vier S). Im Anschluss daran werden die Ergebnisse der S zusammengetragen.
Teilen Sie dann das Arbeitsblatt aus und spielen Sie die Sequenz noch einmal vor. Jetzt können S die Teilaufgabe a) lösen und danach in Partnerarbeit korrigieren.
Bevor die Wochenenderlebnisse von Maya, Greg und Josh gezeigt werden, sollen S Teilaufgabe b) erledigen. Die hierbei entstehenden Ideen können in der Klasse ausgetauscht werden. Zeigen Sie dann den Rest der Sequenz A. S können währenddessen überprüfen, ob ihre Vermutung gestimmt hat und sollen sich zudem merken, wie Maya und Josh ihr Wochenende verbracht haben.

> **Lösung**
> a) 1. *computer games*; 2. *second*; 3. *eleven*; 4. a) *three CDs*; b) *£ 10*
> b) *Individuelle Schülerlösungen*

Worksheet, p. 18

TIPP
Bei Bedarf kann die Höraufgabe durch eine kleine Tabelle vorstrukturiert werden:

	talks about ...
G1:	
G2:	
B1:	
B2:	

Post-viewing

Maya's or Josh's weekend?

In Teil a) tragen S den Anfangsbuchstaben des jeweils passenden Namens vor jedem Satz in der ersten Spalte ein. Lassen Sie S bei der Bearbeitung von Aufgabenteil b) zunächst die einzelnen Stationen von Joshs Tour durch London nummerieren. Es bietet sich an, die sortierte Niederschrift als Hausaufgabe zu geben.

> **Lösung**
> a) M; J; J; M; J; J; M; J; J; M
> b) *Last weekend I went to find some places for my new film about London. First I went to Hyde Park. Then I went to Buckingham Palace. And the Queen was in. After that I went to Trafalgar Square. It was very busy. I also went to Tower Bridge, but it didn't open! And here I am filming the Houses of Parliament across the River Thames. Look, there's Big Ben.*

Worksheet, p. 19

Worksheet, p. 19

My weekend-word puzzle

S erstellen ein Wörterrätsel für ihren Partner/ihre Partnerin. Dazu schreiben sie zunächst zehn Wörter zum Thema Wochenende auf [Teilaufgabe a)].
b) S verteilen die Wörter nun in dem Gitter von links nach rechts (auch diagonal) und von oben nach unten. Der Schwierigkeitsgrad kann noch gesteigert werden, indem Sie Wörter von rechts nach links und von unten nach oben zulassen. Stehen alle zehn Wörter im Gitter, werden die restlichen Felder durch irgendwelche Buchstaben aufgefüllt, die dann keinen Sinn mehr ergeben. S tauschen ihre Rätsel aus [Teilaufgabe c)] und bearbeiten diese mit Zeitvorgabe, z. B. 5 Minuten (gefundene Wörter umkreisen oder mit Farbe markieren). Anschließend werden die Rätsel in Partnerarbeit gelöst.

TIPP
S können hier nur Hauptwörter, nur Verben oder nur Adjektive einsetzen. Eine schwierigere Variante wäre, die zehn Wörter nicht über dem Rätsel, sondern auf einem anderen Blatt zu notieren. S wissen dann nicht, nach welchen Wörtern sie suchen sollen.

2 Unterrichtsvorschläge

B. That's life: The London Eye

Overview

Sequence	Track	Duration	Characters	Storyline
Studio	Track 9	00:21	Dave, Rani	
B: That's life: The London Eye	Track 10	07:08	Maya, Josh, Greg	The three reporters are doing a project on the London Eye for school. First, they surf the Internet to collect information, and a few days later they go on the London Eye. They are very impressed by its size and by the great view they have from their capsule. After their ride they sit down to have lunch, but when Maya and Josh open their bags there is nothing left! Greg has eaten all their food. Maya suggests to go to her house to have a pizza.

Ziele
- über Sehenswürdigkeiten sprechen
- differenzierte Informationen über eine Sehenswürdigkeit heraushören
- selbstständig Informationen über eine Sehenswürdigkeit sammeln

Neuer Wortschatz (2B)
What are … up to?, slow down, dot, flight, plane, big wheel, to cost, each, news, jumble sale, Royal Festival Hall, area, tall, tallest, building, Canary Wharf Tower, far, kilometre, to move, slow, slowly, to go around, it says, guide book, boat, mile, glasses, St Paul's Cathedral, yet, brilliant, Post Office Tower

Pre-viewing

Where are the sights?

Worksheet, p. 20

Beginnen Sie die Arbeit an dieser Videosequenz mit einem Lehrer-Schüler-Gespräch. Ermutigen Sie S, von Sehenswürdigkeiten zu berichten, die sie bereits besucht haben. Fragen Sie: *"Have you ever seen a real famous sight?" "Are there any sights around here?"* S nennen ausländische und regionale Sehenswürdigkeiten, die sie kennen oder vielleicht sogar schon besucht haben. Gehen Sie dann zu den Londoner Sehenswürdigkeiten über, indem Sie S zunächst die Teilaufgaben a) und b) in Einzelarbeit bearbeiten lassen. (Falls Sie die Unterrichtseinheit zu den Sehenswürdigkeiten in London nicht behandelt haben, sollten sie vor Bearbeitung der Aufgabe auf diese eingehen, s. Tipp.) Zur Verdeutlichung können die sich nicht in London befindlichen Sehenswürdigkeiten im Bild durchgestrichen werden. Es sollte kurz darüber gesprochen werden, in welchen Städten die anderen Sehenswürdigkeiten zu finden sind.

TIPP
Falls S die Sehenswürdigkeiten nicht kennen, können Sie sie als Hausaufgabe im Internet oder in Büchern recherchieren und kleine Vorträge vorbereiten lassen.

> **Lösung zu a)**
> a) Sights in London: Big Ben, London Eye, Cutty Sark, Tower of London
>   Not in London: Eiffel Tower (Paris), Colosseum (Rome), Empire State Building (New York), Brandenburger Tor (Berlin)
> b) z. B.: London Dungeon, Madame Tussaud's, Buckingham Palace, etc.

In Teil c) sprechen S in Partnerarbeit darüber, für welche Sehenswürdigkeiten sie sich interessieren und was sie dort gern tun würden. Die vorgegebenen Satzanfänge erleichtern das freie Formulieren.

> **Lösungsvorschlag zu c)**
> *I am interested in the Cutty Sark because I like ships. I think that the Cutty Sark is beautiful. It is a museum now, so I can learn a lot about old ships when I go there. I can also listen to stories about life on the sea, that's fun!*

Teil d) erleichtert S den Überblick über die Stadt und vereinfacht das Nachvollziehen der Fahrt bzw. der Beobachtungen aus der Gondel in der nun folgenden Videosequenz.

TIPP
In leistungsstärkeren Klassen können S im Anschluss an dieses Gespräch der Klasse über die Interessen des Partners/der Partnerin berichten.

Unterrichtsvorschläge 2

While-viewing

The London Eye: Are you a good London guide?

Worksheet, p. 21

Verteilen Sie das Aufgabenblatt und besprechen Sie die Aufgabenstellung mit S, bevor Sie die Sequenz zeigen, damit die Aufmerksamkeit fokussiert wird. Lassen Sie S die Sequenz bei Bedarf zweimal ansehen. Halten Sie das Video an, wenn Maya, Josh und Greg die Gondel betreten und sichern Sie die Ergebnisse der S.

> **Lösung**
> 1. wheel; 2. £6,50; 3. 130; 4. tallest; 5. 40; 6. 8,000; 7. 25

In the capsule: What are they talking about?

Worksheet, p. 21

Zeigen Sie die Szene in der Gondel nun ohne Ton. (Film anhalten, wenn die Teenager die Gondel verlassen.) Lassen sie S anschließend ein mögliches Gespräch in Dreiergruppen aufschreiben. *"What are they talking about in the capsule?"* Dabei übernimmt jede/r S eine der Rollen (Maya, Greg, Josh). Die Gespräche werden zunächst in den Kleingruppen eingeübt, bevor sie dann vor der Klasse vorgespielt werden. Während des Einübens sollten Sie helfend eingreifen, wenn Verständnisschwierigkeiten bzw. gravierende Fehler beim Vorspielen zu erwarten sind. Bei Bedarf kann die Szene nochmals ohne Ton angeschaut werden.
Zeigen Sie nach der Schülerpräsentation dann die Videosequenz mit Ton bis zum Ende.

Post-viewing

Three reporters and their project

Worksheet, p. 21

Hier wird der Inhalt der Sequenz B noch einmal vergegenwärtigt, indem S zunächst die Halbsätze verbinden und im Anschluss daran in der richtigen Reihenfolge aufschreiben. Das Verbinden der Sätze kann in Partnerarbeit erfolgen.

> **Lösung**
> 4.-e; 1.-g; 6.-c; 8.-d; 3.-a; 7.-f; 5.-b; 2.-h

> **TIPP**
> Alternativ zum Schreiben können die Satzteile von S auch ausgeschnitten und in die richtige Reihenfolge gelegt werden. Nach der Ergebnissicherung kleben S den Text in ihr Heft.

Do your own project and create a page for a tour guide

Als Abschluss für *Unit 2* bietet es sich an, S selbst ein Internetprojekt erarbeiten zu lassen. Sammeln Sie zunächst unterschiedliche Recherchemöglichkeiten an der Tafel: *library, magazines, travel brochures, Internet.* Sprechen Sie auch die unterschiedlichen Internet-Suchmaschinen an. Es ist weiterhin sinnvoll, im Vorfeld des Projekts selbst Zeitschriften, Reisekataloge und Reiseführer zu sammeln und S zur Verfügung zu stellen. *Buckingham Palace* eignet sich gut für dieses Projekt, da S sowohl Informationen über das Gebäude selbst als auch über die *Royal Family* sammeln können. Zudem werden die meisten zumindest den Namen schon einmal gehört haben und so Interesse an dem Projekt haben. Teilen Sie die Klasse in Vierergruppen auf und stellen Sie S Overheadfolien, wasserlösliche Folienstifte, große Papierbögen sowie Schere und Klebstoff zur Verfügung. Geben Sie folgende Leitfragen für die Projektarbeit vor:

Where is it? What can you see inside/outside? Can you visit this building? When can you go there? How much is the entrance fee? Which photos can you show?

Nachdem S alle Informationen gesammelt und sich Stichpunkte notiert haben, gestalten sie eine Reiseführerseite, am besten als großes Plakat, die zum Abschluss der Klasse präsentiert wird.
  L *Find out facts about a famous London sight and present your own page for a tour guide to your class.*

> **Lösung**
> *Individuelle Schülerlösungen*

> **TIPP**
> Lassen Sie S nach der Präsentation auch berichten, wie sie ihre Informationen gefunden und zusammengestellt haben. Bei Verwendung von Material aus dem Internet sollten S die Quellen angeben.

17

Unit 2
A. Focus on: The weekend

Pre-viewing

Classroom survey: What did you do last weekend?

a) *Ask three pupils from your class about their weekend and make notes in the grid.*

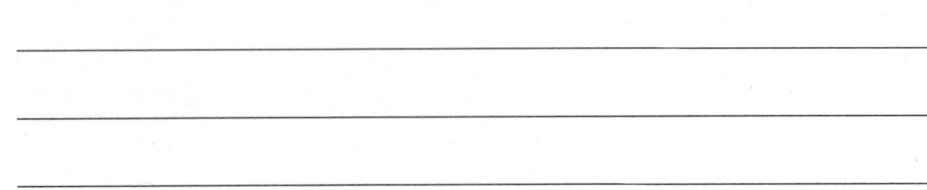

Questions	Name:	Name:	Name:
How was your weekend? Cool or boring, interesting, nice, …?			
Did you stay at home or did you go out last weekend?			
Did you watch TV? How much TV did you watch?			
Did you play computer games? How many hours did you play?			
What else did you do?			

b) *Now tell the class what you know about your classmates' weekend.*

c) *What do you think British teenagers do at the weekend? Write it down in your exercise book.*

While-viewing

What did they do?

a) *Listen carefully, underline the wrong information and correct it.*

1. The first girl has got ten computers. _____

2. 20 people came to the first girl's party. _____

3. The first boy watched 5 hours of TV at the weekend. _____

4. a) The second boy bought a CD player. _____

   b) He gets £20 pocket money. _____

b) *Now look at Greg's Dad. What do you think Greg did at the weekend? Write two or three sentences.*

_____

_____

_____

Post-viewing

Maya's or Josh's weekend?

a) *The two weekends are mixed up! Which sentences are Josh's, which are Maya's? Write M (Maya) or J (Josh) in front of the sentences.*

☐ Emma did my hair. What do you think?!

☐ Then I went to Buckingham Palace. And the Queen was in.

☐ I also went to Tower Bridge, but it didn't open!

☐ On Saturday night I had a sleepover at my house.

☐ Last weekend I went to find some places for my new film about London.

☐ And here I am filming the Houses of Parliament across the River Thames. Look, there's Big Ben.

☐ We didn't go to sleep until three in the morning.

☐ After that I went to Trafalgar Square. It was very busy.

☐ First I went to Hyde Park.

☐ So we didn't get much sleep! On Sunday we were very tired.

b) *Now put Josh's weekend in the correct order and write the sentences in your exercise book.*

My weekend-word puzzle

a) *Write 10 weekend-words on the line.*

_____

_____

b) *Now write your words into the grid (in different directions). After that fill in all the other gaps with senseless/any letters. Only use capital letters!*

c) *Now let a partner find your words.*

2 Worksheet

B. That's life: The London Eye

Pre-viewing

Where are the sights?

a) *Maya, Josh and Greg are surfing the Internet for their project on the London Eye, but the website they have found is about famous sights all over the world! Can you help them? Which sights are in London?*

Sights in London: _____

_____

b) *Which other sights do you know in London?*

_____
_____
_____
_____
_____

c) *Which sights in London would you like to visit? Why? Tell your partner. You can look at the boxes for help.*

I would like to visit … because …		I think that … is nice/ beautiful/interesting
	I'm interested in … because …	I can learn/play/ have fun at/in …

d) *Now look at a map of London. What do you think: Which sights can you see from the London Eye? Talk about it in class.*

_____
_____

Worksheet 2

While-viewing

The London Eye: Are you a good London guide?

Fill in the gaps.

1. The London Eye is a big _____ .

2. A flight costs _____ per person.

3. The London Eye is _____ metres high.

4. It is one of the _____ things in London.

5. You can see for _____ kilometres from the top of the London Eye.

6. In a year it goes around _____ times.

7. One capsule can take _____ people.

In the capsule: What are they talking about?

Find two partners and play the roles: One of you is Maya, one is Josh and one is Greg.

a) *Watch the film without voices and guess what they are saying.*

b) *Write your conversation in your exercise book.*

c) *Practise the scene and play it out in class.*

Post-viewing

Three reporters and their project

Match the first and second part of each sentence. Then put all the sentences in the right order.

1. When they found out the entrance fee	a. at Josh's guide book.
2. They took the next bus into Greenwich	b. he took Maya's and Josh's sandwiches out of their bags.
3. In front of the London Eye they looked	c. but they had to collect old clothes with her for a jumble sale on Saturday.
4. First they surfed	d. Greg said: "Wow, it's so tall!"
5. When Greg was hungry	e. the Internet for information on the London Eye.
6. Josh's Mum bought the tickets,	f. they saw the Houses of Parliament, Buckingham Palace and St. Paul's Cathedral.
7. From the London Eye capsule	g. Josh asked his Mum to buy the tickets for them.
8. When they arrived at the London Eye	h. and had a pizza at Maya's house.

Unit 3
A. Focus on: Fashion

Overview

Sequence	Track	Duration	Characters	Storyline
Studio	Track 13	01:12	Dave, Rani	
A. Focus on: Fashion	Track 14	04:17	Maya, Greg, Josh, two boys and four girls	Greg, Maya und Josh give a report on their favourite clothes and interview kids about what they like to wear.

Ziele
- sich über Mode unterhalten
- Festigung der Relativpronomen *who* und *which*
- Mode beschreiben und eine Modenschau vorführen

Neuer Wortschatz
show, earring, fashion, What on earth …?, coat, totally, shorts, a lot, wicked, sneaker, same, hood, necklace, market, sale, cheap, piercing, to allow, tattoo

Pre-viewing

Fashion: Clothes and things

Worksheet, p. 26

Teil a) der Aufgabe führt S in die Sequenz „Mode" ein. Er dient der Wiederholung des Wortfeldes Kleidung und Accessoires, die in den Teilen b) und c) durch die Verwendung von *who* und *which* vertieft wird (s. Tipp).
Verteilen Sie das Arbeitsblatt. Lassen Sie S die Dinge anmalen, deren Bezeichnung sie auf Englisch kennen. Anschließend schreiben S die Wörter auf und tragen in die Kästchen ein, ob das Kleidungsstück/der Gegenstand typisch für Jungen (B), für Mädchen (G) oder für beide (U = unisex) ist. Teilaufgabe c) soll S motivieren, über die Personen im Film genauer nachzudenken. Sie stellen Vermutungen an, was Maya, Josh und die anderen in dieser Filmsequenz tragen werden, notieren Stichpunkte zu den einzelnen Personen und formulieren anschließend ganze Sätze im Heft.

TIPP
In leistungsschwächeren Gruppen sollten die folgenden beiden Sätze als Muster vorgegeben werden, damit S ihre weiteren Aussagen strukturieren können:
Greg is a person who often wears shorts and T-shirts, so I think that he is wearing shorts and a T-shirt in this unit.
Or: *Shorts and T-shirts are things which Greg often wears, so I …*
S schreiben ihre Lösungssätze ins Heft.

Lösung
a) + b) + c) Individuelle Schülerlösungen

While-viewing

Friends and fashion

Worksheet, p. 27

Erläutern Sie S die Aufgabenstellung. Spielen Sie dann den ersten Teil der Filmsequenz (bis zum Schnitt zu *Vox pops*) zweimal vor. Während des Sehens schreiben S die gesuchten Begriffe auf die Schreiblinien. Anschließend wird die Lösung besprochen, indem jeweils zwei S die Lieblingskleidung von Greg und Josh beschreiben.

Lösung
Greg: caps and hats, long hair, shorts, sneakers; Josh: caps and hats, short hair, shoes

What do they like to wear?

Worksheet, p. 27

S setzen sich mit dem Rücken zum Fernsehgerät. Zeigen Sie nun den zweiten Teil der Sequenz *(Vox pops)*. S hören zu und versuchen möglichst viele Wörter und Informationen zum Thema Mode/Kleidung aufzunehmen und in ihrem Heft zu notieren.

Ergänzen Sie solche Informationen, die S zu diesem Zeitpunkt noch nicht versprachlichen können, da einige Wörter hier neu eingeführt werden (z. B. *hood, stuff, sale, piercing*).

S sehen nun den Film, ordnen die Personen den passenden Sprechblasen zu und finden den korrekten Wortlaut der Aussagen der befragten Jugendlichen. Zeigen Sie abschließend diesen Kurzausschnitt zur Überprüfung ein weiteres Mal.

> **Lösung**
> a) A–3; B–2; C–1; D–5; E–6; F–4.
> b) 1. skirts and jeans; 2. sweatshirts; 3. trainers; 4. piercings or tattoos; 5. clothes; 6. another piercing, earrings

Post-viewing

My favourite clothes

Worksheet, p. 27

In dieser Aufgabe sollen S zunächst ihre Lieblingskleidungsstücke bzw. Accessoires ausschneiden und aufkleben. Ein solcher Arbeitsauftrag spricht viele S besonders an und ist vor allem den Mädchen durch die Eintragungen in ihre „Freundschaftsbücher" vertraut. Aber auch vielen Jungen dieses Alters ist es nicht mehr gleichgültig wie sie aussehen. Dennoch sind einige Jungen noch weniger modebewusst. Weisen Sie diese S darauf hin, dass auch Greg seine Lieblingssachen anhat, die ja nicht unbedingt modisch sind.

In ihren Texten beschreiben S dann ihre Lieblingskleidung und sagen, wann sie welche Kleidung gerne tragen und ggf. auch, mit wem sie zum Einkaufen gehen. Weisen Sie S darauf hin, dass sie auch Aussagen zu Kleidungsstücken machen können, die sie überhaupt nicht mögen bzw. die sie niemals anziehen würden.

Die Miniposter können entweder zu einer Art Modegalerie oder aber zu einem Modekatalog der Klasse zusammengestellt und im Klassenraum ausgehängt bzw. zusammengeheftet werden.

> **Lösung**
> *Individuelle Schülerarbeiten*

TIPP
Informieren Sie S etwa eine Woche vor dem Zeigen der Sequenz, dass sie alte Modezeitschriften, Kataloge oder Werbeprospekte aus der Tageszeitung mit Mode mitbringen sollen. Sammeln Sie selbst auch solches Material für S, die in der betreffenden Stunde ihre Zeitschriften vergessen haben.

Project: Fashion show

Geben Sie Mayas und Joshs Fragen *Do you follow fashion? What do you and your friends wear – at school and at home?*, die die beiden Reporter am Ende der ersten Sequenz stellen, an S weiter. Sammeln Sie die Antworten an der Tafel und helfen Sie ggf. bei Wortschatzproblemen. Lassen Sie S anschließend in Kleingruppen besprechen, was sie als Model auf einer Modenschau von ihren persönlichen Kleidungsstücken vorstellen würden. In der Hausaufgabe fertigen S einen beschreibenden Text über dieses ‚Outfit' an, den L Korrektur liest. In Zusammenarbeit mit dem Fach Kunst können Werbeplakate für die Veranstaltung gestaltet werden und auch eine Vorführung vor größerem Publikum, etwa im Pädagogischen Zentrum der Schule, kann angedacht werden.

Am Tag der Modenschau führen S dann diese Kleidungsstücke auf dem Klassenlaufsteg vor. Lassen Sie S wie richtige Models über den *Catwalk* schreiten und ‚ihre Mode' vorstellen. Zur Untermalung wird passende Musik von CD eingespielt und aussprachesichere S (oder aber L) trägt wie bei einer echten Modenschau den Beschreibungstext für das gespannte Publikum vor. Die Zuschauer sollten wohlwollend applaudieren. Ein besonderer Höhepunkt ist es, wenn auch Sie ihre Lieblingsmode auf dem Laufsteg präsentieren.

Wenn Sie einen Computerraum zur Verfügung haben, können Sie nach der Modenschau von jedem S ein Digitalfoto machen. S gestalten am Computer eine Seite mit ihrem Foto und ihrem Text. Diese Seiten können zu einem kleinen Büchlein zusammengefasst und für alle S vervielfältigt werden – nach Möglichkeit in Farbe.

TIPP
Für die Durchführung der Modenschau in der Klasse sollte eine ganze Unterrichtsstunde vorgesehen werden, da sich erfahrungsgemäß viele S, und nicht nur die Mädchen, vor dem Auftritt umziehen und herrichten möchten.

3 Unterrichtsvorschläge

B. That's life: Friends?

Overview

Sequence	Track	Duration	Characters	Storyline
Studio	Track 15	00:40	Dave, Rani	
B. That's life: Friends?	Track 16	03:05	Maya, Maya's mum and dad, Stacey (Maya's little sister)	Stacey's family notices a bad scratch on her arm. At first Stacey refuses to say what happened, but later in her room she confesses to Maya that she has been bullied by a girl at school because of her trainers. Maya offers help, but Stacey sorts it out alone and the 'bully' and Stacey are friends again.

Ziele
- über ein Problem (*bullying*) sprechen
- Festigung des *simple past*, auch mit Fragen und Verneinungen
- Dialoge rekonstruieren

Neuer Wortschatz
should, upset, arm, nothing, Leave me alone., love, accident, Jemma, horrible, bush, bully, jealous, needn't worry, texting, or else, myself, to hurt

Pre-viewing

What is going on here?

Diese Aufgabe dient der Einstimmung der S auf die Ausgangssituation der Videosequenz, in der Stacey verärgert und gekränkt ist. S sollen sich hier in Staceys Gefühlslage versetzen.
Kopieren Sie ein Foto oder eine Zeichnung eines enttäuschten Jugendlichen (Jugendmagazin) mittig auf eine Folie. Lassen Sie S in einem ersten Schritt spontan sagen, wie sich die dargestellte Person(en) wohl fühlen mag und mögliche Gründe hierfür nennen.
Sprechen Sie in einem zweiten Schritt S direkt an und lassen Sie sie über ihre eigenen Erfahrungen oder die Erfahrungen anderer berichten. Zeichnen Sie hierzu Linien auf die Folie, die von dem Bild ausgehen und geben Sie folgende Satzanfänge vor:
I was upset when …; My brother/sister was upset when …; My friend xxx was very upset when …; My parents were very upset when …; Xxx was upset when …
Weisen Sie S darauf hin, dass die Sätze im *simple past* beendet werden sollen.
Ggf. können S auch kurze Texte schriftlich anfertigen.

TIPP
Kopieren Sie in leistungsschwächeren Gruppen die Zeichnung oder das Foto und die Satzanfänge auf ein Arbeitsblatt mit Schreiblinien und lassen Sie die einzelnen Sätze lediglich beenden. Leistungsstarke S werden eine Geschichte erzählen wollen. Hier sollten S eine Person, über die sie erzählen möchten, auswählen.

L *Think about a time when you, your family, your friends or your teachers were upset and tell stories about it.*

While-viewing

Diese Übung dient dem genauen Zuhören und Zuschauen. Zeigen Sie die gesamte Filmsequenz einmal. Besprechen sie dann erst die Aufgabenstellung. Weisen Sie S nachdrücklich darauf hin, dass sich die zu lösende Aufgabe von Szene zu Szene verändert. So müssen S in Szene 1 die vorgegebenen Aussagen Staceys an die richtige Stelle des Dialogs setzen. In Szene 2 sollen S Details der Aussagen aus der Videosequenz als falsch erkennen und korrigieren. Weisen Sie S darauf hin, dass sich in jede Äußerung jeweils nur ein Fehler – insgesamt 15 (!) – eingeschlichen hat. Bei der Aufgabe zu Szene 3 müssen S genau hinschauen und zuhören, um herauszufinden, wer die Sätze spricht und in welcher Reihenfolge sie gesagt werden.
Präsentieren Sie den Film nun szenenweise ein zweites Mal. S lösen die jeweilige Aufgabe während des Zusehens und vergleichen anschließend ihre Ergebnisse. Beim dritten Sehen überprüfen S ihre Lösungen und korrigieren sie in Partnerarbeit.

Worksheet, p. 28

Worksheet, p. 29

> **Lösung**
> *Scene 1:* What? – It's n-nothing. Leave me alone. – It's just a scratch, OK? – Leave me alone, can't you? – I told you, it was an accident, OK!
> *Scene 2:* 1. brother = sister; 2. earrings = trainers; 3. big boys = little girls; 4. do = say; 5. listen = talk; 6. great = cool; 7. girl = friend; 8. lose = win; 9. look = laugh; 10. cry = worry; 11. writing = doing; 12. an e-mail = a message; 13. sending = texting; 14. monster = sister; 15. play with = talk to
> *Scene 3:* 5 (Stacey) – 6 (Maya) – 3 (Stacey) – 2 (Mum) – 1 (Stacey) – 7 (Stacey) – 4 (Maya)

Post-viewing

Let's act

Worksheet, p. 29

Fordern Sie die S auf Gruppen zu bilden und die Rollen zu verteilen. Zeigen Sie den Film ein weiteres Mal. Weisen Sie S darauf hin, dass sie genau auf die Intonation, Mimik und Gestik der Person achten müssen, deren Rolle sie im folgenden Spiel übernehmen werden. S üben dann den Dialog (s. Filmskript ab S. 67) ein. Gehen Sie herum und helfen Sie bei Aussprache- bzw. Betonungsproblemen. S lernen ihre Rolle auswendig und spielen die Szenen in der folgenden Stunde nach. Ermuntern Sie die Kinder ihr Vorspiel ‚in Szene zu setzen', indem sie Requisiten (etwa: ein auffälliges Paar Turnschuhe, eine Sporttasche, ein Handy, usw.) für ihren Auftritt mitbringen und sich ggf. auch ansatzweise als ‚Mum'/‚Stacey'/‚Maya'/‚Dad' verkleiden. Die Gruppen spielen nacheinander die kurzen Szenen vor der Klasse vor.

L a) *Get together in groups, please. Decide who is going to play Stacey, Maya, etc.*
   b) *Watch the film. Then learn and act the scenes in your group.*

Alternativ – etwa in großen Lerngruppen oder aus Gründen der Zeitökonomie – können Sie die Sequenz auch in die drei Teilszenen unterteilen. Demnach üben je drei S die Szene 1 und 3 ein, und zwei S proben in Partnerarbeit die Szene 2. Zum Vorspiel finden sich dann zehn S zu einer großen Gruppe zusammen und spielen die gesamte Sequenz mit fliegendem Wechsel der Akteure vor.

Let's talk: Bullies

Im Anschluss an die Filmsequenz können Sie S noch die Möglichkeit geben, über ihre eigenen Erfahrungen mit dem Thema *bullying* zu sprechen. Da viele S dieser Altersgruppe bereits damit in Kontakt gekommen sind, wird es ihnen nicht an Ideen fehlen, sich hier mündlich zu äußern. Ein Problem könnte die sprachliche Umsetzung sein. Geben Sie ggf. Satzanfänge vor, mit deren Hilfe S ihre Geschichte erzählen können, oder stellen Sie Fragen, die S beantworten können *(What happened? When did it happen? Where did it happen? Who was with you/your friend? What did the bully (bullies) want? What did she/he/they say? What did you/your friend say/do? How did you/your friend feel? What did you/your friend do later? Was that a good way to react? Or are there better ways?).*
Erarbeiten Sie abschließend von der Frage *What can you do if someone bullies you?* ausgehend Vorschläge, wie sich S in solch einer Situation verhalten können. Etwa:

- tell your parents/brother/sister
- tell a teacher
- tell your friend(s)
- talk to a nice girl/boy in your class
- you can laugh
- show that you are not scared or upset

S sollte hierbei noch einmal bewusst werden, dass sie auch in der Schule in einer Gemeinschaft leben, in der es auf gegenseitige Rücksichtnahme, die Beachtung von Regeln und Kooperation ankommt.

L a) *Do you or your friend know about a bully? What did he/she do? Say what happened.*
   b) *What can you do when someone bullies you?*

> **TIPP**
> Das Auswendiglernen kann in die Hausaufgabe verlegt werden. Da hier fast immer nur Mädchen mitspielen möchten und Jungen sich oft scheuen, Mädchenrollen zu übernehmen, könnten die Namen verändert werden. Aus *Maya* wird *Greg* (der auch einen kleinen Bruder hat) und aus *Stacey* wird *Ron*. Die Rollen von *Mum* und *Dad* können zusammengelegt werden. Im Text müssten dann einige Stellen verändert werden, z.B. könnte *Jemma Jim* genannt werden.

> **TIPP**
> Besprechen Sie im Vorfeld, welche Requisiten real vorhanden sein sollten.

> **TIPP**
> Sammeln Sie mit S die häufigsten Formen des *bullying* im Vorfeld: *taking money from younger children, beating up smaller kids, using horrible words/calling kids names, threatening to give a secret away, making them do things they do not want to, e.g. the bullies' homework, telling stories.*

Unit 3
A. Focus on: Fashion

Pre-viewing

Fashion: Clothes and things

a) *Colour the things that you know the English word for.*

b) *Write down the names of the things for boys* B *, for girls* G *, or for boys and girls* U

_____ ☐   _____ ☐   _____ ☐   _____ ☐

_____ ☐   _____ ☐   _____ ☐   _____ ☐

_____ ☐   _____ ☐   _____ ☐   _____ ☐

_____ ☐   _____ ☐   _____ ☐   _____ ☐

_____ ☐   _____ ☐   _____ ☐   _____ ☐

c) *What do you think Rani, Dave and the three reporters are wearing in this film? Write down your ideas. Your words from b) can help you.*

Rani: _____

Dave: _____

Maya: _____

Josh: _____

Greg: _____

Worksheet 3

While-viewing

Friends and fashion

Josh and Greg are good friends but they don't like all the same things. Watch and write down what they like.

GREG

_____

_____

_____

JOSH

_____

_____

_____

_____

What do they like to wear?

a) *Who says what? Draw a line between the pictures and the right sentences.*

b) *What do they say? Underline the right words.*

1. I really like skirts and jeans/shirts and jeans/skirts and shirts but anything really.

2. I like trainers/T-shirts/sweatshirts … with a hood.

3. I like T-shirts/trainers/trousers like these.

4. No, I don't like earrings or tattoos/piercings or tattoos/earrings or piercings.

5. I spend most of my pocket money on T-shirts/sweatshirts/clothes.

6. I wanted a necklace/another piercing/pink trainers but my parents said no. I'm only allowed white trainers/blue jeans/earrings!

Post-viewing

My favourite clothes

From magazines and brochures cut out the things you like to wear and stick them on a worksheet. Then write a text about your favourite clothes and where you like to wear them.

3 Worksheet

B. That's life: Friends?

While-viewing

Scene 1: In Maya's kitchen

What does Stacey say? Choose sentences from the box that go with the text first. Write them on the lines. Then watch the film and check if your ideas are correct.

| It's just a scratch, OK? Leave me alone, can't you? | | What? |

| | I told you, it was an accident, OK! | | It's nothing. Leave me alone. |

Mum: What's that, Stacey?

Stacey: _____

Mum: There's a red scratch on your arm! Here, let me have a look.

Stacey: _____

Mum: Let me see. It's a scratch! And it looks very red.

   What happened, Stacey?

Stacey: _____

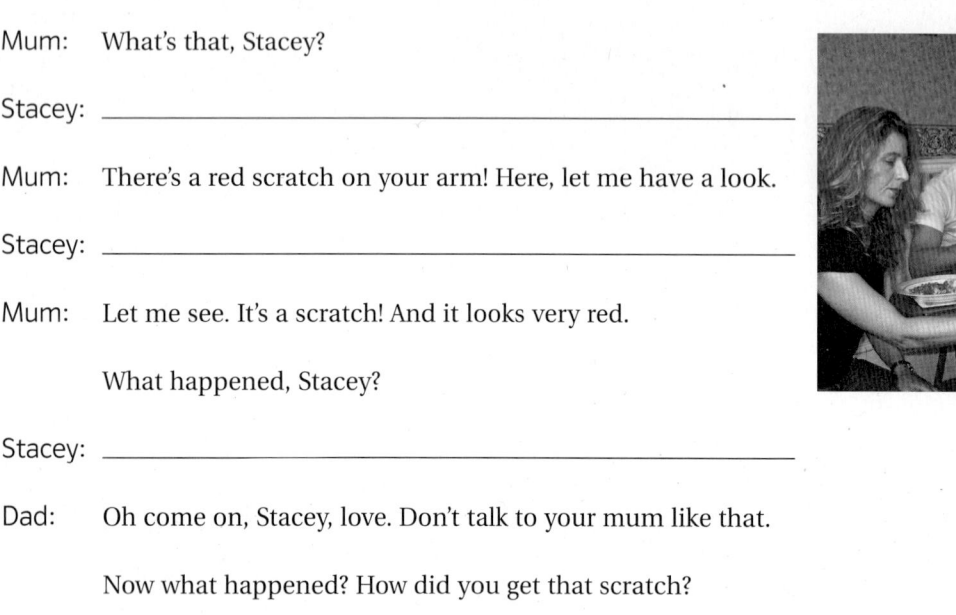

Dad: Oh come on, Stacey, love. Don't talk to your mum like that.

   Now what happened? How did you get that scratch?

Maya: Yeah, did it happen at school, Stacey?

Stacey: _____

Scene 2: In Stacey's bedroom

There are a lot of mistakes in the text. What do Maya and Stacey really say in this scene? Cross out the wrong words and write the correct words.

Maya: It wasn't an accident, was it, Stacey? What happened?

   You can tell me. I'm your ~~brother.~~ sister

Stacey: It was Jemma! She's being horrible to me! In PE, she made fun

   of my earrings, said they were silly.

Stacey: She said they're for big boys, babies! And then she threw them

   behind the bush.

Maya: What did you say then?

28

Stacey: I got them but I scratched my arm on the bush. Then I went over to sit with my friends to listen to them.

Maya: Good! That was the right thing to do! That Jemma's a bully! Your new trainers are great. She's just jealous. I'm sure she really wants a pair just like yours.

Stacey: She was my best girl! I'm not wearing those again!

Maya: You must wear them, Stacey! You can't let that bully Jemma lose!

Stacey: But I don't want her to look at me again.

Maya: Hmmm. You needn't cry.

Stacey: W-what are you writing?

Maya: I'm sending Jemma an e-mail!

Stacey: A message? What are you sending?

Maya: Leave … my … little monster … alone. … Or else …!

Stacey: No – don't do that! Thanks, Maya. But I must play with Jemma myself.

Scene 3: In Maya's kitchen later that week

Watch the film and find out who says what. Then find the right order of the sentences.

_____ : Of course. ☐

_____ : And did you see that big bully Jemma? ☐

_____ : Cool! ☐

_____ : Hi! How was school? ☐

_____ : Hiya! ☐

_____ : Jemma? Oh yeah! She's OK really! We're friends again! And do you know what? She's got some trainers just like mine! ☐

_____ : So Stacey! Did you wear your new trainers today? ☐

Post-viewing

Let's act

Work in groups. You are Stacey, Maya, Mum and Dad. Read the dialogues. Then learn and act the scenes with your partners.

Unit 4
A. Focus on: Music

Overview

Sequence	Track	Duration	Characters	Storyline
Studio	Track 19	00:49	Dave, Rani	
A. Focus on: Music	Track 20	05:30	Greg, Maya, Josh and kids in the street	Greg, Maya and Josh talk about their favourite music and interview kids in the street about what they like to listen to and where they get their music from.

Ziele
- sachbezogenen Wortschatz sammeln
- über Musik sprechen
- eine Radioshow erstellen und durchführen

Neuer Wortschatz
rock, heavy metal, track, others, reggae, to prefer, classical, rock 'n' roll, Elvis, king, American, to become, even if, tour, private, autograph, to take photographs, hip hop, punk, best, open air, mate, noisy, difference

Pre-viewing

Music, music, music

Worksheet, p. 34

Diese einleitende Übung dient der Festigung der Schreibung und beugt den Verständnishürden vor, die vielleicht beim Sehen des Videos entstehen könnten.
Zunächst umkreisen S die 18 verborgenen Wörter, die fast alle aus der Arbeit mit dem Lehrbuch/Film bekannt sind bzw. durch Ähnlichkeiten oder Parallelen mit dem deutschen Sprachgebrauch (etwa: *concert* oder die gängigen Bezeichnungen der Musikrichtungen wie *pop*, *rock'n'roll* oder *hiphop*) eigenständig erschlossen werden können. Die nicht benutzten Buchstaben müssen so angeordnet werden, dass der Name eines bekannten Sängers als Lösungswort erscheint. Anschließend Besprechung der Lösung im Plenum, Notieren der gefundenen Wörter auf den vorgegebenen Schreibzeilen und Überleitung zur ersten Filmsequenz.

TIPP

Kopieren Sie das Wortsuchrätsel auf eine Folie, auf der S die Lösungswörter mit einem löslichen Folienstift umkreisen. Da einige Wörter in einem *word search* anders geschrieben werden müssen, sollten Sie die problematischen Wörter ergänzend in ihrer richtigen Schreibung an der Tafel notieren.

Lösung

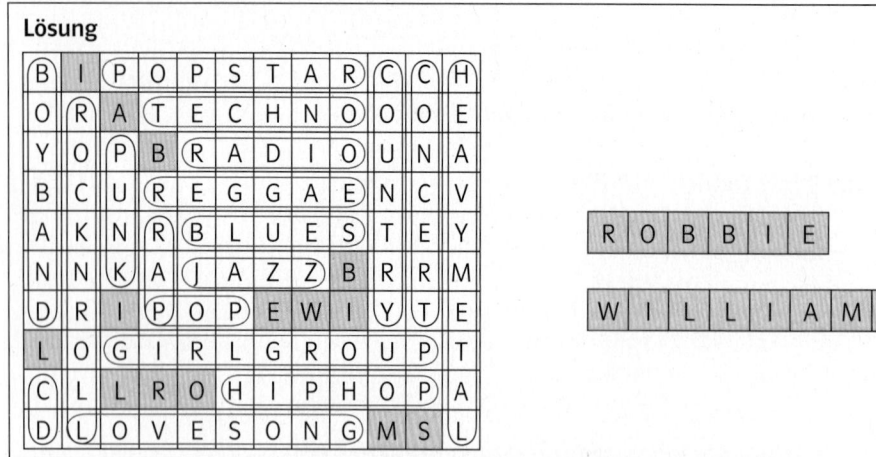

While-viewing

Musical reporters

Worksheet, p. 34

Erläutern Sie die Aufgabenstellung und sagen Sie, dass Maya, Greg und Josh über ihre *favourite music* berichten werden. Lassen Sie S die Aussagen lesen und Vermutungen darüber anstellen, welcher der drei Reporter hier gemeint sein könnte und warum.

Zeigen Sie dann den ersten Teil der Filmsequenz bis Greg sagt: *OK ... cut!* S ordnen während des Sehens die Aussagen den Personen zu, indem sie die Anfangsbuchstaben des jeweiligen Namens eintragen und so die Richtigkeit ihrer Vermutungen überprüfen.

> **Lösungsvorschlag**
> M: *dances to girl group music.*
> J: *likes hip hop, reggae and classical music.*
> G: *likes heavy metal, of course!*
> G: *sings 'Hounddog' like Elvis Presley.*
> J: *plays air violin.*
> M: *likes girl groups and boy bands.*
> G: *plays air guitar.*
> M: *would like to be on the TV show 'Popstars'.*
> J: *dances to reggae music.*

That's our music

Worksheet, p. 35

Zeigen Sie nun den zweiten Teil der Filmsequenz. S kreuzen die Sätze an, die für den jeweiligen Interviewpartner zutreffend sind. Betonen Sie, dass mehrere Sätze richtig sein können. Danach sehen S diesen Teil ein zweites Mal und überprüfen die Ergebnisse.

> **Lösungsvorschlag**
> 1. a), b); 2. c); 3. a), c); 4. b), c).

Words – words – words

Worksheet, p. 35

Während sie die gesamte Filmsequenz noch einmal sehen, sammeln S die Musik-Wörter aus dem Film und ergänzen weitere Musikbegriffe. Einige Wörter werden von Maya, Josh und Greg in dieser Sequenz genannt, andere sind S aus ihrer eigenen Beschäftigung mit populärer Musik bekannt. Hier werden S vermutlich Wörter wählen, die zu ihrem eigenen Musikstil passen. Sie sammeln so Vokabular, das sie anschließend in der *post-viewing*-Phase verwenden können.

> **TIPP**
> Legen Sie einige Wörterbücher bereit, damit S, falls erforderlich, nachschlagen können. Vervielfältigen Sie die korrigierten Ergebnisse, so dass S eine große Anzahl von Wörtern zum Wortfeld Musik zur Verfügung steht.

Post-viewing

Talk about your music

Fordern Sie S auf, ihre Lieblingsmusik (Stilrichtung, Interpreten, Radio-/TV-Musiksendungen) kurz vorzustellen. Hierzu können Bilder und Fakten auch im englischsprachigen Internet gesammelt werden. Anschließend kann das Material ggf. auf ein Poster aufgeklebt werden. In leistungsstärkeren Lerngruppen können S kleine Kurzreferate vorbereiten und diese vortragen.

Can you play my music? – A request programme

Worksheet, p. 35

Besprechen Sie die Arbeitsschritte mit S und übernehmen Sie während der Gruppenarbeitsphase die Rolle des Beraters/der Beraterin. S sollten bei dieser Aufgabe ihre Partner/innen selbst wählen dürfen, da beim Thema Musik der Geschmack der S weit auseinander geht. Bereiten Sie S darauf vor, dass sie tolerant genug sein sollten, den Gruppen auch dann aufmerksam zuzuhören, wenn die „Wunschmusik" nicht ihrem Geschmack entspricht, da jede Gruppe gearbeitet und das Recht auf eine ungestörte Präsentation ihrer Radioshow hat.
Da S dazu tendieren, einmal geschriebene Texte bei der Präsentation abzulesen, sollten sie sich von Anfang an daran gewöhnen, möglichst frei zu sprechen. Weisen Sie S darauf hin, dass auch geübte Sprecher in Funk und Fernsehen zwar Karten haben, auf denen Notizen stehen, dass aber ein freier Vortrag immer interessanter für die Zuhörer ist. Alle Mitglieder der Gruppe sollten Sprechanteile haben, die mimisch und gestisch untermalt werden. Geben Sie eine maximale Spielzeit vor, für diese Altersgruppe maximal 5–8 Minuten, um die Präsentationen nicht ausufern zu lassen.

> **Lösung**
> *Individuelle Schülerlösungen*

4 Unterrichtsvorschläge

B. That's life: Star Reporters

Overview

Sequence	Track	Duration	Characters	Storyline
Studio	Track 21	00:37	Dave, Rani	
B. That's life: Star Reporters	Track 22	05:28	Maya, Josh, Greg, Tess	Maya, Josh, Greg and Tess are practising for an audition. Maya, their lead singer, gets upset because she thinks they have got the wrong song, the wrong clothes and the wrong band name. When the others don't agree with her, she storms out of the room but comes back the following day and apologizes. In the meantime she has found new clothes for the band. She also admits that Greg's song and their name 'Star Reporters' are OK. She even knows the text of the song by heart.

Ziele
- über einen Konflikt sprechen und Lösungen finden
- Festigung des Wortschatzes zum Thema music
- ein Klassenprojekt planen und durchführen

Neuer Wortschatz
argument, keyboard, guitarist, lead singer, drummer, personality, to pass, ourselves, to look, except, stupid, to give it a try, to run off

Pre-viewing

What's going to happen?   Worksheet, p. 36

Zeigen Sie die einleitende Studioszene bis Dave sagt: *"All those different personalities. Have a look."* Unterbrechen Sie den Film an dieser spannungsaufbauenden Stelle und nutzen Sie den Schnitt vom Studio hin zum Probenraum der *Thomas Tallis School* für Hypothesenbildungen durch S. Kopieren Sie hierzu ggf. das Poster aus der Aufgabe 1 auf eine Folie. S besprechen in Partnerarbeit ihre Vermutungen über den Inhalt der folgenden Filmsequenz und notieren Stichwörter. Sammeln Sie einige Schüleraussagen unkommentiert auf der Folie oder an der Tafel. Nach der *While-viewing*-Phase können Sie gemeinsam mit S überprüfen, welche Vermutungen über den Verlauf der Filmszene zutreffend waren.

L *Look at the poster. What is going on at Thomas Tallis School?*
What do you think Maya, Josh and Greg are doing in the film?

> **Lösung**
> *Individuelle Schülerlösungen*

While-viewing

In the school band room – 'before' and 'after'   Worksheet, p. 36

Lassen Sie S, bevor sie die Sequenz vorspielen, die Aufgabenstellung durchlesen. S notieren während bzw. unmittelbar nach dem Sehen des Films Stichwörter zu den beiden Fotos, die sie behalten haben. Vor allem in lernschwächeren Gruppen empfiehlt es sich, die Präsentation des Films zwischen den beiden Szenen für einige Minuten zu unterbrechen, damit S in Ruhe ihre Notizen vervollständigen können. Zeigen Sie die Sequenz noch einmal vollständig. S ergänzen bzw. korrigieren ihre Eintragungen. Besprechung und Ergänzung der Schülerlösungen im Plenum.

TIPP
Erweiterung: Teilen Sie das kopierte Skript dieser Sequenz aus. S lernen eine der Rollen auswendig, dann wird die Szene nachgespielt. Tess kann von

Unterrichtsvorschläge 4

Im anschließenden b)-Teil der Aufgabe fassen leistungsstärkere S den Inhalt der beiden Szenen an Hand der Notizen mündlich zusammen. Leistungsschwächere Lerngruppen erhalten die Zusammenfassung der ersten Szene als Lückentext:
Greg, Maya, Josh and their friend Tess want to go to an audition with their (band). They meet in the (school band room) to practise. Greg plays the (guitar), Tess (the) drums and (Josh) the keyboards. (Maya) is their lead singer. Maya is not (happy) because she does not (like the song) which (Greg) has written. She also thinks they are all wearing (stupid clothes). When the others say that she is (not right), she (runs out of the room).

Dieser Text gilt dann als Modell für einen kurzen Text zur zweiten Szene, den S analog gestalten. Diese Aufgabe ist auch als schriftliche Hausaufgabe geeignet.

L *Watch the film and try to remember as many words and phrases as you can.*

> einem/-r leistungsschwächeren S dargestellt werden kann. Diese Rolle könnte jedoch auch sprachlich erweitert werden. S dieser Altersgruppe verkleiden sich gern. Bitten Sie die Gruppen, entsprechende Kleidung zu der Vorführung vor der Klasse mitzubringen.

Lösung
a)+b) Individuelle Schülerlösungen

Post-viewing

How do they feel?

Worksheet, p. 37

In Teil a) dieser Übung verbalisieren S das, was sie im Video gesehen haben und ordnen diese *feeling words* den einzelnen Charakteren zu. Es sind absichtlich mehr Adjektive als Charaktere gegeben. Partnerarbeit ist möglich. Die Ergebnissicherung kann mit Hilfe einer Folie erfolgen.
Der b)-Teil der Aufgabe zielt auf das eigene Erleben der S ab. Schwächere Gruppen werden die Sätze lediglich beenden, stärkere S sollten ermuntert werden, die jeweilige Situation etwas genauer zu beschreiben. Es ist durchaus denkbar, dass S auch eine Geschichte erzählen wollen. Diese Variante ist erwünscht.
Aufgabenteil c) zielt auf Konfliktlösungsstrategien ab, die S hier verbalisieren sollen. S lernen, dass es nicht ausreicht, sich nur zu entschuldigen, wenn man „schlechte Laune" hatte. Sie sehen an Mayas Beispiel, dass man eigene Fehler erkennen und auch zugeben sollte, und dass es sich lohnt, wenn man sich Verbesserungsvorschläge überlegt. Stärkere Gruppen lösen diese Aufgabe ohne Hilfe des Lehrers, in schwächeren könnten für die einzelnen Schritte Satzanfänge vorgegeben werden (vgl. Lösung).

> **TIPP**
> Lassen Sie S eine Geschichte schreiben, in der sie mindestens sechs der Adjektive verwenden.

Lösungsvorschlag
a) 1. astonished; 2. upset; 3. surprised; 4. happy;
b) Individuelle Schülerlösungen
c) 1. Maya brings cool new clothes for the band. 2. Maya says sorry to the group. 3. Maya tells Josh that she thinks their name is OK and that she was just upset about the song the day before. 4. Maya tells Greg that she likes his song and that she knows it now.

Do a class project: Pop stars – Your own karaoke show

Worksheet, p. 37

Dieses Projekt zeichnet sich dadurch aus, dass ein erheblicher Teil der Projektarbeit in eigener Regie der S nach dem Unterricht in der Schule bzw. zu Hause erledigt wird.
L bespricht zu Beginn die Arbeitsschritte mit S, legt den Zeitrahmen fest und bestimmt, welche Räumlichkeiten von S benutzt werden können, damit die einzelnen Gruppen ungestört an ihren Projekten arbeiten können. Notfalls kann auch mit Kopfhörern, am Nachmittag und/oder zu Hause gearbeitet werden.
Für die Aufführung in der Klasse sollte eine eigene Unterrichtsstunde eingeplant werden. L und S entscheiden gemeinsam, ob und in welcher Form die Show ggf. auch außerhalb der eigenen Klasse vorgestellt wird. Auch die Möglichkeit einer Videoaufzeichnung sollte erwogen werden.

> **TIPP**
> Führen Sie eine Wahl (ähnlich zu bekannten TV-Sendungen wie *Pop stars/DSDS* durch. Die besten Gruppen werden prämiert. S geben zu diesem Zweck ihr Urteil ab, z.B. durch Lautstärke und Länge des Applauses oder die Vergabe von Punkten. L und eine S-Jury entscheiden.

Lösung
Individuelle Schülerlösungen

Unit 4
A. Focus on: Music

Pre-viewing

Music, music, music

Find 18 music words (↓ →). Draw a circle around the words and write them in the list. Work with a partner. There are 14 extra letters. They make the name of a famous British pop singer.

B	I	P	O	P	S	T	A	R	C	C	H
O	R	A	T	E	C	H	N	O	O	O	E
Y	O	P	B	R	A	D	I	O	U	N	A
B	C	U	R	E	G	G	A	E	N	C	V
A	K	N	R	B	L	U	E	S	T	E	Y
N	N	K	A	J	A	Z	Z	B	R	R	M
D	R	I	P	O	P	E	W	I	Y	T	E
L	O	G	I	R	L	G	R	O	U	P	T
C	L	L	R	O	H	I	P	H	O	P	A
D	L	O	V	E	S	O	N	G	M	S	L

While-viewing

Musical reporters

Who does or likes what? Fill in the names.

_____ dances to girl group music.

_____ likes hip hop, reggae and classical music.

_____ likes heavy metal – of course!

_____ sings 'Hounddog' like Elvis Presley.

_____ plays air violin.

_____ likes girl groups and boy bands.

_____ plays air guitar.

_____ would like to be on the TV show 'Popstars'.

_____ dances to reggae music.

That's our music

Tick ✓ the right sentence(s) that go(es) with the pictures. One, two or three sentences can be right.

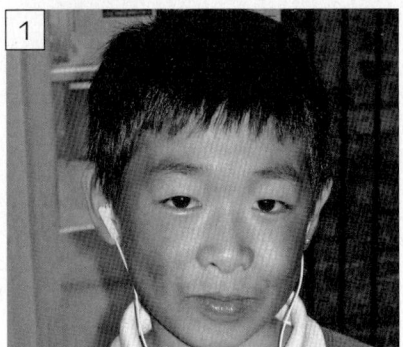

a) ☐ He likes rock music.
b) ☐ He has got an MP3 player.
c) ☐ He never goes to concerts.

a) ☐ She likes hip hop best.
b) ☐ She likes to watch music videos on TV.
c) ☐ She buys CDs or gets them from friends.

a) ☐ She listens to the radio.
b) ☐ She likes open air concerts.
c) ☐ She likes all kinds of music.

a) ☐ He likes punk and rap music.
b) ☐ He downloads songs.
c) ☐ He doesn't go to concerts.

Words – words – words

Watch and listen again. Write down all the music words that you hear in the film. Add more music words.

Post-viewing

Can you play my music? – A request programme

You want to make your own radio programme? Here is what to do.
- Get into groups. In your groups find names for your radio station and your programme and think of names for the presenter(s) of your phone-in show.
- Talk about who in your group does what. (e.g.: Who is/are the presenter(s)/the caller(s)?/ Who plays the music/records the songs which you need for your programme?)
- Discuss these questions:
  – How does the presenter/do the presenters start the show?
  – How does she/he tell the listeners to phone in? (Don't forget to give them a telephone number!)
  – How does the presenter/do the presenters end the show?
  – What props do you need for show?
- Write down dialogues between the callers and the presenter(s).
- The listeners can also text messages, send e-mails or fax their music requests. Use these messages for your show.
- Practise your programme. Do it in an empty classroom (or at home). Make sure that you speak loud enough.
- Present your request show in class.

4 Worksheet

B. That's life: Star Reporters

Pre-viewing

What's going to happen?

Look at this poster. Something is going to happen at Thomas Tallis School. But what? And what are our reporters doing in this episode? Make notes and then talk about your ideas with a partner.

_____
_____
_____
_____
_____
_____

While-viewing

In the school band room – 'before' and 'after'

a) Watch the film and collect words and phrases. Write down keywords only.

Before: _____

_____
_____
_____

After: _____

_____
_____
_____
_____

b) With the help of your notes try to say what happened in the school band room.

_____
_____
_____

36

Worksheet 4

Post-viewing

How do they feel?

a) *Choose adjectives from the right that go with the pictures. You can use a dictionary for help.*

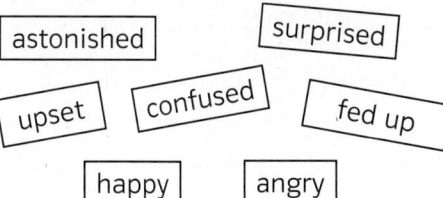

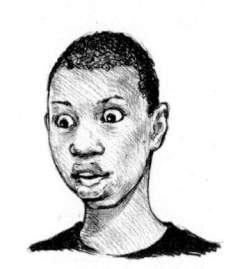

astonished · surprised · upset · confused · fed up · embarrassed · happy · angry

_____   _____   _____   _____

b) *What about your feelings? Use adjectives from a) and finish the sentences.*

1. I am always _____ when _____

2. I was _____ because/when _____

3. I often feel _____ when _____

4. I have often been _____ because/when _____

5. I'll never feel _____ when _____

6. I felt _____ when _____

c) *What does Maya do to say sorry? Write it down in your exercise book.*

1 · 2 Sorry! · 3 OK. · … our name? · Good. · … the song? · 4

Do a class project: Pop stars – Your own karaoke show

Make your own class karaoke show and find out who are real pop stars in your class.
- Get into groups. In your group find a song which most of you like.
- Find the lyrics (= the text) and an instrumental version of your song.
- In a dictionary, find the words from the text which you do not know and make sure that you know how to say the new words. Do not forget to ask your teacher if you need help.
- In your group, talk about who does what:
  – Who is going to sing which part of the song?
  – Are you going to sing your part alone or together with a partner?
- Listen to your song a few times and practise your part. Sing it in different ways (loud, soft, funny, …).
- Think about some good movements for your hands, arms, legs, body, eyes, … .

Unit 5
A. Focus on: Healthy food

Overview				
Sequence	Track	Duration	Characters	Storyline
Studio	Track 25	01:18	Dave, Rani	
A: Focus on: Healthy food	Track 26	07:06	Greg, Josh, Maya	In the first part of this sequence Josh and Maya explain which food and drinks you should choose if you want to have a healthy lunch. In the second part Greg shows how to make a vegetable curry, a healthy and popular meal. In the last part, Maya tells the story of how curry came to Britain.

Ziele
- gesundes und ungesundes Essen unterscheiden und benennen können
- ein in Großbritannien sehr bekanntes und beliebtes Gericht und dessen Herkunft kennen lernen
- Festigung des Wortschatzes zum Thema *food*

Neuer Wortschatz
to not feel so good, cheeseburger, muffin, coke, to feel ill, health, fitness, energy, body, canteen, smokey bacon, salt, vinegar, salted, onion, Help yourself., still, fizzy, can (Dose), pardon me, human body, at least, litre, to stand by, chef, dish, powder, hot, delicious, garlic, carrot, something else, ladies' fingers, to chop, vegetarian, meat, colony, a long time, all over Britain, village

Pre-viewing

What is good for you? Worksheet, p. 42

a) S beschriften die einzelnen Lebensmittel in Einzelarbeit. Nach einer kurzen Ergebnissicherung bearbeiten S Aufgabenteil b) wahlweise in Einzel- oder Partnerarbeit. Falls S zusammenarbeiten, sollten ihnen Redemittel (über Tageslichtprojektor oder Tafel) zur Verfügung gestellt werden: *"I think ... is good for you/healthy/…"*

> **Lösung**
> *Healthy food: carrots, apples, bananas, oranges, salad, water, cheese, fish*
> *Unhealthy food: chips, chocolate, crisps, coke, hamburgers, muffins*

TIPP
Es bietet sich an, ein bzw. mehrere Wortfelder zum Thema *food* erstellen zu lassen. So kann bereits bekannter Wortschatz reaktiviert werden und neue Wörter können strukturiert ergänzt werden (gut als Hausaufgabe denkbar).

Für die Diskussion in Teil c) steht S nun Wortschatz für gesunde bzw. ungesunde Lebensmittel zur Verfügung. Leiten Sie die Diskussion ein, indem Sie über Ihre eigenen Essgewohnheiten sprechen. Übergeben Sie dann an S, die sich gegenseitig befragen.

L *I like chocolate best. It's unhealthy. But I also like healthy things, like salad and fish. What do you like best, Paul?*
S1 *I like chips best. They're unhealthy. What do you like best, Sophie?*
S2 *I like cheese best. It's healthy.*

Teilaufgabe c) sollte im Plenum durchgeführt werden.

While-viewing

Do Josh and Greg like healthy food? Worksheet, p. 42

Lassen Sie S die Sequenz einmal lediglich unter der Fragestellung der Überschrift (ohne Aufgabenblatt) anschauen. Teilen Sie nun die Aufgabe aus. S dürfen die Bilder ansehen und, wenn sie es schon wissen, das richtige Tablett einkreisen. Nun zeigen Sie den Film ein zweites Mal, dabei kreisen S die entsprechenden Lebensmittel ein.

> **Lösung**
> *Josh's lunch is on tray 1: fresh salad, cake, banana, fizzy drink, water*
> *Greg's curry: potatoes, curry powder, onions, garlic, ladies' fingers, rice, salt*

Can you help Maya?

Worksheet, p. 43

Die Übung sollte zunächst in Einzelarbeit erledigt werden. Falls dies zu schwierig sein sollte, kann dieser Teil der Sequenz nochmals gezeigt werden bzw. die Übung in Partnerarbeit gemacht werden. Eine weitere Hilfe wäre das Angeben des jeweils ersten Wortes im Satz.

> **Lösung**
> 1. *India was a British colony for a long time.*
> 2. *When the British left India they brought curry back to Britain.*
> 3. *Later many Indian people came to live in Britain.*
> 4. *Some Indians opened curry restaurants called 'curry houses'.*
> 5. *Today you can find curry houses all over Britain.*
> 6. *Curry has become Britain's favourite food.*

Post-viewing

My favourite meal

Worksheet, p. 43

S zählen in Teilaufgabe a) auf, was Bestandteile ihres Lieblingsessens sind. Legen Sie dazu, wenn möglich, Wörterbücher aus, damit unbekannte Wörter von S selbstständig nachgeschlagen werden können. Für die Erledigung dieser Aufgabe ist es nicht wichtig, dass S das Gericht kochen können oder alle einzelnen Zutaten kennen. Lediglich die wichtigsten und erkennbaren Bestandteile sollen genannt werden, damit auch das Erraten durch den Partner in Teilaufgabe b) nicht zu schwierig wird.

Möglicher Dialog:
S1 *The first thing is a vegetable. You must cry when you chop it.*
S2 *Onion!*
S1 *That's right. The second thing is also a vegetable. Inside it is yellow and outside it is brown …*
S2 *A potato!*
…

> **TIPP**
> Alternativ besteht die Möglichkeit, S zunächst die Definitionen in ihr Heft schreiben zu lassen, bevor sie diese jemandem vorstellen (Gefahr: eher Ablesen anstatt freie und spontane Kommunikation).

> **Lösung**
> *Individuelle Schülerlösungen*

A typical German meal

Worksheet, p. 43

Lernstärkere Gruppen können hier einen freien Text gestalten, indem sie über ein typisch deutsches Gericht schreiben oder über ein in Deutschland beliebtes Gericht, das aber seinen Ursprung in einem anderen Land hat wie z. B. Döner, Gyros, Pizza.

> **Lösung**
> *Individuelle Schülerlösungen*

B. That's life: Fit – fitter – the fittest

Overview

Sequence	Track	Duration	Characters	Storyline
Studio	Track 27	00:36	Dave, Rani	
B. That's life: Fit – fitter – the fittest	Track 28	06:30	Greg, Josh, Maya, Greg's mum	The three reporters talk about the different kinds of sport they do and who is the fittest. Each of them thinks that her/his sport is the best exercise. To find out who is really the fittest, Maya suggests they have a competition. They start with Greg's sport, football, go on with badminton, Josh's favourite, and finally the boys have to do aerobics. In the end the boys give in and agree that Maya is the fittest.

Ziele
- Über Sport sprechen und Wortschatz dazu reaktivieren und erweitern
- Rollen übernehmen und sich in die Lage Anderer versetzen

Neuer Wortschatz

to exercise, jazz dance, class, aerobics, on your marks … get set … go, anyone, serious, to hit, lady, alright, tiring, whatever, Get on with it!, to give in, rest

Pre-viewing

Sports

1. *What comes into your mind when you think of sports?*
   S werfen sich einen Ball (oder ein Indiaca o.ä.) zu. Wer den Ball hat, sagt spontan drei Dinge, die mit dem Thema Sport zu tun haben. Neben Sportarten können auch andere Substantive (*goalkeeper, runner, tennis racket, gloves, sports bag, etc.*) oder auch Verben *(to run, to throw, to dance, etc.)* und Adjektive *(stressful, tiring, exciting, etc.)* genannt werden. Das gegenseitige Zuhören kann gesteigert werden, indem Doppelnennungen nicht vorkommen dürfen.
2. *What do you think: What kind of sport do our reporters like? Talk to your partner.*
   S stellen nun Hypothesen über die Lieblingssportarten der Reporter auf und sprechen darüber zunächst in Partnerarbeit. Danach befragen Sie S zu den Ergebnissen ihrer Partnergespräche.

> **TIPP**
> Alternativ können S vor dieser Übung zunächst ein individuelles schriftliches *brainstorming* (in Einzelarbeit) in ihr Heft schreiben.

While-viewing

Who says that?

Worksheet, p. 44

Lassen Sie S nun die Sequenz vollständig ansehen. Im Anschluss daran teilen Sie ihnen diese Aufgabe aus. Einige Namen können von S sicherlich nach dem ersten Anschauen eingetragen werden. Bei Bedarf kann die Sequenz ein zweites Mal angesehen werden. Dabei können S die Aufgabe vervollständigen.

> **Lösung**
> 1. Maya; 2. Greg; 3. Josh; 4. Maya; 5. Greg; 6. Maya; 7. Greg; 8. Greg; 9. Josh; 10. Greg

An dieser Stelle können bei Bedarf die Hypothesen der S in der *pre-viewing*-Aufgabe 2. nochmals thematisiert und richtig gestellt werden.

> **Lösung**
> Maya likes aerobics, Greg likes football, Josh likes badminton.

Unterrichtsvorschläge 5

What do Maya, Josh and Greg think?

Worksheet, p. 44

Nachdem S nun die Einstellungen und Äußerungen von Maya, Josh und Greg kennen gelernt haben, sollen sie sich nun überlegen, was die Drei in den verschiedenen Momenten wohl denken. Die Bilder sollen die Kreativität der S anregen. Da die Einstellungen der Charaktere zu den einzelnen Sportarten mittlerweile klar sind und auf den Bildern durch Mimik und Gestik unterstrichen werden, können S hier entweder bereits Bekanntes anwenden oder aber ganz neue Gedanken mit einbringen.

> **Lösungsmöglichkeiten**
> *Bild 1: Greg: This is silly. Football is much more fun. Josh: I'm a cool aerobic-rapper. Maya: They will be so tired in a minute!*

Post-viewing

Sport words

Worksheet, p. 45

S bilden Wortfelder für verschiedene Sportarten. Dabei dürfen nur die Wörter aufgeschrieben werden, die einen Buchstaben der jeweiligen Sportart enthalten. Geben Sie hierzu folgendes Beispiel:

```
        R  E  F  E  R  E  E
              O
              O  G     A  L
H  A  L  F  T  I  M  E
              B
           C  H  A  M  P  I  O  N  S  H  I  P
        B  A  L  L
              L
```

> **TIPP**
> S schreiben anschließend ihre eigene Lieblingssportart von oben nach unten und finden dazu passende Wörter von links nach rechts.

Geben Sie vor, ob S jeweils drei, fünf oder so viele Wörter wie möglich finden sollen. Zur Unterstützung können Wörterbücher ausgelegt werden. Durch die Vorgabe eines Zeitlimits kann die Übung als kleiner Wettbewerb durchgeführt werden: *How many words can you find in three minutes?* (Oder: Wer zuerst je drei Wörter gefunden hat, hat gewonnen.) Falls Zweifel darüber bestehen, ob das Wort wirklich zur jeweiligen Sportart gehört, hat S die Möglichkeit, den eigenen Gedankengang auf Englisch zu begründen.

> **TIPP**
> Als Hausaufgabe eignet sich auch das Erstellen eines Textes/Posters/einer *mindmap* zum Thema *My favourite sport*.

> **Lösungsmöglichkeiten**
> *Basketball: player, basketball shoes/trainers, court, NBA, ball*
> *Tennis: table, racket, net, lines*
> *Dancing: dress, pop star, dancer, music, video*

Who am I?

Worksheet, p. 45

S übernehmen die Rolle eines von ihnen gewählten bekannten Sportlers. Sie schreiben eine Beschreibung des Stars in der Ich-Form auf das Aufgabenblatt. Weisen Sie darauf hin, dass die Sprachhilfen in der Box verwendet werden können, aber nicht müssen. Geben Sie S den Tipp, am Anfang nicht gleich so viele Informationen zu geben, dass die Mitschüler/innen später den Star gleich nach einem Satz erraten. Und: Keiner darf die Lösung wissen, auch nicht der Nachbar oder die Nachbarin!
Zur Durchführung des Ratespiels teilen Sie die Klasse in zwei Mannschaften. Nacheinander treten S vor die Klasse und tragen ihre Informationen vor. Die Mannschaft, die den Sportler/die Sportlerin zuerst errät, bekommt drei Punkte. Um zu vermeiden, dass S einfach Namen herausrufen, verteilen Sie für falsche Antworten jeweils einen Minuspunkt. Die Punkte sollten für alle ersichtlich, z.B. an der Tafel, festgehalten werden. Falls das Rätsel nach dem Kurzvortrag noch nicht gelöst werden kann, dürfen die Mannschaften abwechselnd Fragen an den Star stellen, die dieser mit Ja/Nein beantworten kann.

> **TIPP**
> Falls es eventuell weniger sportbegeisterten S schwer fällt über einen Star zu schreiben, kann die Aufgabe auch in Partnerarbeit erledigt werden. (Dann zwei Stars beschreiben, so dass jede/r S eine Rolle hat.)

Unit 5
A. Focus on: Healthy food

Pre-viewing

What is good for you?

a) *What food can you see in the pictures?*

b) *Which food is good for your body and which is not? Cross out the unhealthy food.*

c) *Tell your partner what you like to eat. Discuss if the things you like are healthy or not.*

While-viewing

Do Josh and Greg like healthy food?

Which lunch belongs to Josh? Circle the correct tray.

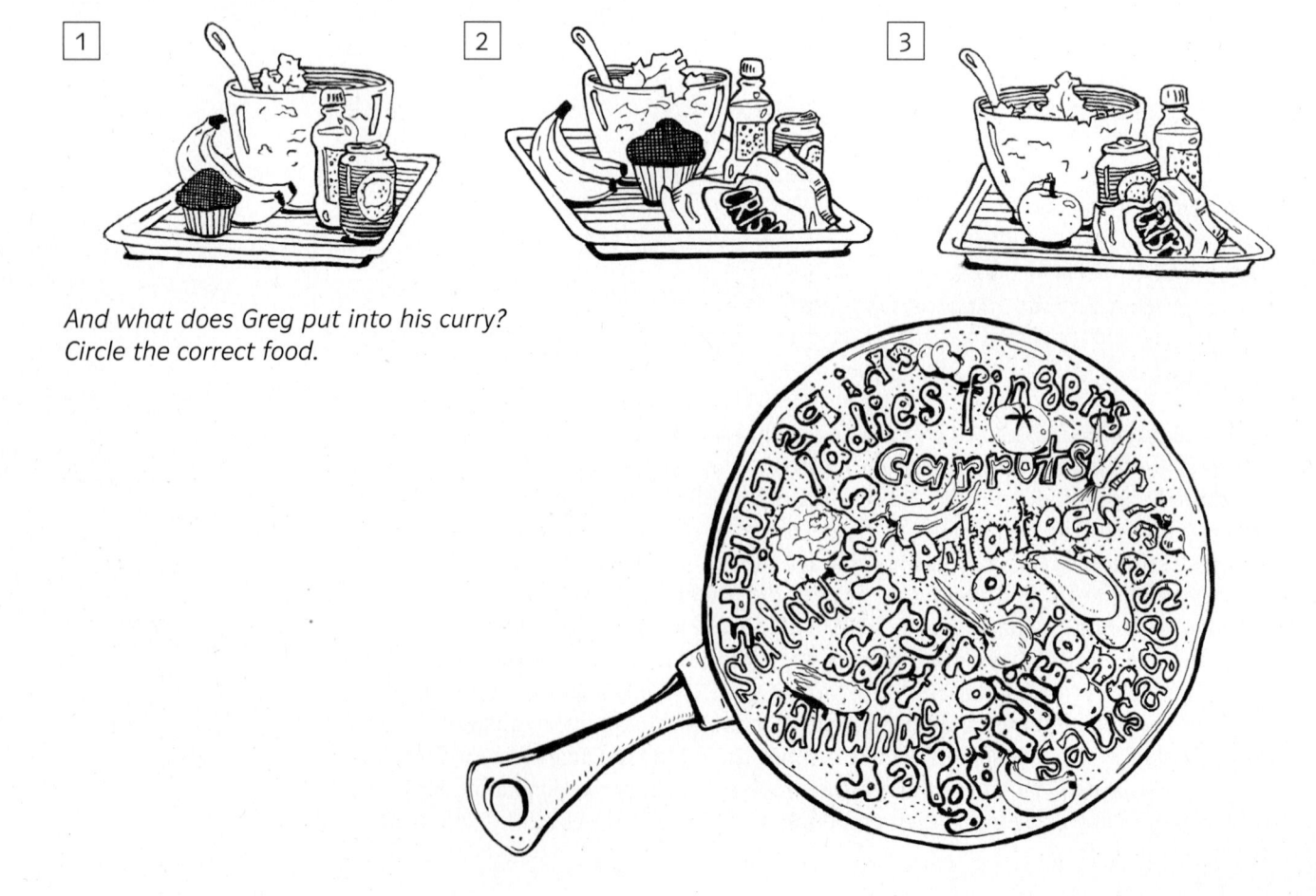

1   2   3

And what does Greg put into his curry?
Circle the correct food.

Worksheet 5

Can you help Maya?

Maya has written down the story of curry, but Greg and Josh have mixed up all the sentences! Please help her to put the words into the right order and write down the correct sentences.

1. was/India/for a long time/a British colony

   _____

2. India/curry/when/to Britain/left/they/the British/brought/back

   _____

3. many/later/came to live/Indian people/in Britain

   _____

4. opened/called/Indians/some/curry restaurants/'curry houses'

   _____

5. can find/all over Britain/curry houses/today/you

   _____

6. favourite/has become/food/Britain's/curry

   _____

Post-viewing

My favourite meal

a) *My favourite meal is* _____

   Write down what you need to make it: (If you don't know the words, use a dictionary.)

   _____

b) Talk to your partner: Describe five things which are in your favourite meal but don't say these words!
   (For example: "A vegetable that makes you cry when you chop it." → onion)
   Your partner guesses the words. Can he/she find out your favourite meal?

A typical German meal

Write five sentences about a typical/popular meal in Germany.

_____

_____

_____

_____

_____

5 Worksheet

B. That's life: Fit – fitter – the fittest

While-viewing

Who says that?

Look at the sentences. They are all from the video. But who says them? Write down the right names after the sentences.

1. Who knows, Greg, maybe your mum is fitter than you! _____
2. I'm much fitter than my mum. _____
3. I'm fit because I play badminton. _____
4. Let's see who is really the fittest. We could have a kind of competition. _____
5. On your marks, get set, go! _____
6. Footballers are fitter than I thought. _____
7. Badminton is more tiring than football! _____
8. Stop, Maya! I've had enough! I give in! _____
9. You win, badminton isn't as tiring as aerobics. _____
10. Maya, you're the fittest! _____

What do Maya, Josh and Greg think?

What do the people in the pictures think? Write it in the bubbles.

Worksheet 5

Post-viewing

Sport words

Find words that go/(have s.th. to do) with the sport and write them from left to right.

	B	A	L	L			T				D			
F	A	N					E				A			
	S						N				N			
	K						N				C			
	E						I				I			
	T						S				N			
	B										G			
	A													
	L													
	L													

Who am I?

Think of a famous sports star. Imagine you are him or her! Later your classmates must find out who you are, so you must give them some information about yourself.

You can use this box or …

I was born in (country) _____

I am _____ cm tall and have _____ hair.

I am good at _____

I like _____

For my sport I need a _____

I often do my sport with _____

… you can write your own text:

I'm a man/a woman and … _____

_____

_____

Unit 6
A. Focus on: Broughton Castle

Overview

Sequence	Track	Duration	Characters	Storyline
Studio	Track 31	00:55	Dave, Rani	
A. Focus on: Broughton Castle	Track 32	06:08	Maya, Greg, Josh, Josh's mum, Lord Saye	Josh, Greg and Maya do a report about Broughton Castle. They show different places in and outside the castle and explain how to have a traditional English cream tea. In the end they meet the owner of the castle, Lord Saye.

Ziele
- Landeskunde: eine englische Burg kennen lernen
- anhand von Leitfragen einen Text verstehen
- über eigene Erlebnisse berichten

Neuer Wortschatz
Broughton Castle, owner, Lord, Lady, Saye, Shakespeare in Love, to roll, Great Hall, armour, heavy, arms, sword, to bet, tea room, advert, Kellogs, cornflake, Christmas, to smell, roast, turkey, Christmas pudding, flower, walled garden, traditional, cream tea, to cut in half, strawberry, jam, thick, clotted cream, to leave, to let

Pre-viewing

My home is a castle
Worksheet, p. 50

Kopieren Sie das Portrait von Lord Saye auf Folie und erzählen Sie S, dass er noch heute mit seiner Familie in einem Schloss in England wohnt. Da das Schloss der Öffentlichkeit zugänglich ist und dort auch ab und zu Filme und Reportagen gedreht werden, hat Joshs Mutter an Lord Saye geschrieben und um einen Besuchstermin gebeten. Lord Saye hat tatsächlich zurückgeschrieben…. Teilen Sie nun das Arbeitsblatt aus und lassen Sie S den Brief in Stillarbeit lesen und anschließend die Fragen beantworten.

> **Lösung**
> 1. Lord Saye has written this letter.
> 2. Because Josh's mum is interested in the castle.
> 3. Broughton Castle is about 90 miles north west of London.
> 4. The castle is more than 700 years old.
> 5. They want to meet them on August 21st at 2 o'clock.

While-viewing

Broughton Castle
Worksheet, p. 50

Fragen Sie S, welche Räume man ihrer Meinung nach in einem Schloss bzw. in einer Burg finden kann. Sammeln Sie die Begriffe an der Tafel und teilen Sie dann die Aufgabe aus. Erklären Sie, dass auf den vier Bildern einige der Räume in *Broughton Castle* zu sehen sind. S sollen während des Anschauens der Sequenz die entsprechenden Räume unter die Bilder schreiben und in den Aussagen die falschen Wörter durchstreichen. S sollten kurz Zeit haben die Aussagen durchzulesen, bevor der Film läuft.

Unterrichtsvorschläge 6

> **Lösung**
> 1. Great Hall; falsche Wörter: watched, doesn't like, Maya
> 2. Dining room; falsche Wörter: films, never, gardens
> 3. Castle gardens; falsche Wörter: Greg, toilet
> 4. Tea rooms; falsche Wörter: lemon, butter

Post-viewing

Have you ever visited a castle?

Mit dieser Übung sollen die Erlebnisse der S bezüglich Schlössern (und Burgen) mit einbezogen werden und zugleich eine Erwartungshaltung für das Kommende geschaffen werden. S erzählen sich mit Hilfe der Fragen in der Tabelle in Kleingruppen (vier S), welche Schlösser sie besucht haben, wo diese sind, was ihnen daran gefallen hat, etc. Die Zuhörer schreiben Stichwörter in ihre Tabelle. Achten Sie darauf, dass in jeder Gruppe ein bis zwei S sind, die bereits ein Schloss besichtigt haben. Um später ein möglichst freies Sprechen vor der Klasse zu gewährleisten, sollen S nur einzelne Schlüsselwörter und keine ganzen Sätze schreiben.

Nachdem die Unterhaltung in den Kleingruppen abgeschlossen ist, bitten Sie einzelne S, vor der Klasse anhand ihrer Stichwörter über einen Schlossbesuch eines Klassenkameraden/einer Klassenkameradin zu berichten. Alternativ kann das Gruppengespräch und das Sammeln von Stichwörtern im Unterricht stattfinden. Zu Hause fertigen S dann kurze Texte von sechs bis zehn Sätzen an, die sie in der Folgestunde im Plenum vortragen.

Worksheet, p. 51

> **TIPP**
> Falls sehr wenig S über einen Schloss-/Burgbesuch berichten können, sollte eine Phase dazwischen geschoben werden, in der sie sich über verschiedene Schlösser und Burgen informieren können (Internet, Broschüren, Bücher, etc.). Im Anschluss daran geben S ihre Informationen dann in den Kleingruppen weiter.

> **Lösung**
> *Individuelle Schülerlösungen*

Would you like to live in the past?

Fragen Sie S in Anlehnung an das Filmende, ob sie gerne in der Vergangenheit leben würden. *Would you like to live in the past? Why? Why not? What would you miss?* Das Gespräch kann im Klassenverband oder in Partnerarbeit geführt werden.

> **TIPP**
> Für eine ausführlichere Bearbeitung dieser Frage bietet es sich an, S in einer Tabelle zunächst die Unterschiede von früher zu heute festhalten zu lassen.

Christmas dinner with Lord and Lady Saye

Worksheet, p. 51

S schreiben ein mögliches Gespräch bei einem Weihnachtsessen des Ehepaars Lady und Lord Saye in Dialogform (direkte Rede). Dabei können sie zwei bis drei weitere Gäste erfinden. Falls es S schwer fällt, eine Ausgangssituation zu wählen, sammeln Sie mit ihnen gemeinsam mögliche Gäste (z.B. weitere Familienmitglieder, Maya, Josh, Greg, andere Adelsgäste, etc.) und Sprechanlässe (Essen, Geschenke, Erlebnisse, etc.). Die Szene kann in Einzel- oder Partnerarbeit erstellt werden. Für das Einüben der Szenen finden S sich in Kleingruppen möglichst entsprechend der Anzahl ihrer Charaktere zusammen (vier oder fünf S). Dort tragen sie sich ihre Gespräche gegenseitig vor und einigen sich dann gemeinsam auf eines, das dann einstudiert wird. (In dieser Phase sollten Sie darauf achten, dass keine gravierenden Fehler einstudiert werden.) Fordern Sie S auf, für das Vorspielen vor der Klasse Requisiten zu benutzen.

6 Unterrichtsvorschläge

B. That's life: A trip to the seaside

Overview

Sequence	Track	Duration	Characters	Storyline
Studio	Track 33	00:39	Dave, Rani	
B. That's life: A trip to the seaside	Track 34	06:41	Greg, Josh, Maya, Greg's dad	Greg's dad takes the three reporters to Southend. He wants to spend his day fishing on the pier and hopes to catch lots of fish for tea. In the meantime, the kids go to Adventure Island (a fun park) and have fun on the beach. Unfortunately, Greg's dad doesn't catch any fish, so in the end they get dinner from a fish and chip shop.

Ziele
- Landeskunde: einen britischen Badeort kennen lernen
- Festigung des Wortschatzes zum Thema *At the seaside*
- Nacherzählen eines Erlebnisses (Festigung des *simple past*)

Neuer Wortschatz
at the seaside, lucky things, Southend, pier, along, further, longest, almost, to catch, caught, at the front of, Have fun!, Adventure Island, rock, receipt, all the way through, yummy, to look after, fine, ride, Yikes!, freezing, to expect, bait, to be afraid, single, fun park

Pre-viewing

Where are we going today?

Bringen Sie Gegenstände mit, die Sie mit ans Meer nehmen würden oder die man dort finden kann. (Badeanzug, Schaufel, Muschel, Sand, Sonnencreme, Handtuch, Sonnenhut, Buch, Ball, etc.) Packen Sie die Gegenstände nacheinander aus und fragen Sie S, wo Maya, Josh und Greg wohl heute hingehen.
Nachdem S das Thema erraten haben, können Sie sie fragen, ob sie schon einmal am Meer waren. Lassen Sie S berichten, wo sie waren und was sie dort gemacht haben.

Let's go to the seaside! *Worksheet, p. 52*

Erzählen Sie S, dass Maya, Josh und Greg eine Liste geschrieben haben mit Dingen, die sie mit ans Meer nehmen möchten. Die Wörter sind allerdings etwas durcheinander geraten. Teilen Sie dann das Aufgabenblatt aus und lassen Sie S Teilaufgabe a) in Einzelarbeit bearbeiten. Durch die Bildunterstützung werden S relativ schnell auf die ersten sechs Wörter kommen. Wenn die restlichen vier Wörter schwierig herauszufinden sind, fordern Sie S auf, darüber nachzudenken, was sie selbst mitnehmen würden. Dadurch reaktivieren S ihren Wortschatz zum Thema. Weitere Hilfsmöglichkeit: Sie können die Wörter umschreiben oder von S umschreiben lassen.

Lösung
sandwich, water, crisps, mobile phone, bag, ball, sunglasses, sunhat, money, pullover

While-viewing

What are they doing? *Worksheet, p. 52*

Erklären Sie S kurz die Ausgangssituation: Gregs Vater fährt mit Maya, Josh und Greg ans Meer.
Lassen Sie S die sechs Fotos anschauen. S sollen sich dann umdrehen, sodass sie den Film nicht sehen, sondern nur hören können. Zeigen Sie nun die Sequenz. Danach können S sich wieder umdrehen.

Zur gemeinsamen Ergebnissicherung kopieren Sie die Fotos am besten auf Folie und schneiden sie aus. Lassen Sie S die richtige Reihenfolge legen, anschließend wird mit dem Arbeitsblatt verglichen.

> **Lösung**
> E1, A2, B3, F4, D5, C6

Bevor S die Sequenz nun anschauen, sollten sie kurz Zeit haben, die Lückensätze durchzulesen. Während S den Film sehen, füllen sie die Lücken aus.

Worksheet, p. 53

> **Lösung**
> 1. boy, walk; 2. longest, train, fun; 3. look around, cool; 4. little sister, say, way; 5. last, photos; 6. fish, boy, fish, chips, waiting

Post-viewing

Greg's e-mail to his friend Peter

Worksheet, p. 53

S sollen sich in Gregs Rolle versetzen und den Tag am Meer aus seiner Sicht erzählen. Hierzu schreibt Greg eine E-Mail an seinen Freund Peter. Weisen Sie S darauf hin, dass in einer Nacherzählung das *simple past* benutzt wird. Um sich die Ereignisse des Tages in Erinnerung zu rufen, verweisen Sie S auf die Bilder und Aussagen der vorangegangenen Aufgabe. Leistungsstärkere S können aufgefordert werden, auch über Gregs eventuelle Gedanken zu schreiben, z.B. dass es ihm peinlich war, dass sein Vater keinen Fisch gefangen hat, etc.
Da es sich um eine E-Mail handelt, kann der Text dafür typische Zeichen enthalten und auch etwas umgangssprachlicher formuliert sein.

> **TIPP**
> Falls Sie feststellen, dass S Probleme mit der Verwendung des *simple past* haben, lassen Sie sie alle Verben in ihrer E-Mail unterstreichen und in Partnerarbeit nochmals auf Richtigkeit überprüfen.

> **Lösungsvorschlag**
> Today my Dad took Maya, Josh and me on a trip to the seaside. He wanted to catch a lot of fresh fish for tea. So he stayed at Southend Pier while we went to other places. First we walked along the pier. I didn't like that at all :-(. But we took the train back – Yippie! I liked Adventure Island and playing on the beach but the water was freeeeezing! Maya bought us some Southend Rock which was yummy!!
> At 5.30 we met my Dad again at the pier, and he looked very unhappy! He didn't catch any fish, and we were so hungry! First I was really mad with him but then he had a good idea :-)!! He took us to a nice fish and chip shop and we had a great meal. So we were all happy again.

Die E-Mails können nach Fertigstellung und eventueller Korrektur laut vorgelesen werden. Eine weitere Möglichkeit wäre, die E-Mails mehrmals weiterzugeben und in Stillarbeit lesen zu lassen, was authentischer für eine E-Mail ist.

My holiday in ...

Lassen Sie S ein Strandfoto aus einer Zeitschrift oder aus einem Prospekt mitbringen. Denkbar ist auch die Verwendung eines eigenen Strandbildes. S schreiben zu diesem Bild eine kurze, freie Geschichte.
Alternativ kommen alle mitgebrachten Materialien in einen Pool und werden zugelost. S schreiben eine kurze, erfundene Geschichte.

Unit 6
A. Focus on: Broughton Castle

Pre-viewing

My home is a castle

This is Lord Saye. He lives in a famous castle in Great Britain, and he has written a letter to Josh's mum. Read the letter and answer the questions in complete sentences.

Dear Madam,
Thank your for your interest in Broughton Castle. The castle is very old: more than 700 years old. Lots of films have been made here: 'Shakespeare in love' is one you maybe know. Certainly your son Josh and his friends can do a report about our home. We would like you to visit us on August 21st at 2 o' clock. Broughton Castle is about 90 miles north west of London.

Yours faithfully,
Lord and Lady Saye
Broughton Castle

1. **Who** has written this letter? _____
2. **Why** has he written this letter? _____
3. **Where** is Broughton Castle? _____
4. **How old** is Broughton Castle? _____
5. **When** do they want to meet Josh's mum and the reporters? _____

While-viewing

Broughton Castle

Here you can see some of the rooms and places at Broughton Castle. Find out their names and write them under the pictures. Then cross out the wrong words in brackets.

a) This is where they watched / filmed 'Shakespeare in Love'.
b) Greg likes / doesn't like the arms.
c) Greg / Maya wants to see the dungeon.

a) They sometimes make adverts / films here.
b) The family still / never use this room.
c) Greg wants to go to the gardens / tea rooms now.

a) Greg / Maya likes the garden.
b) Greg runs to the toilet / tea rooms.

a) In England you drink tea with lemon / milk.
b) You put butter / cream on your scone.

Worksheet 6

Post-viewing

Have you ever visited a castle?

Talk to 3 or 4 other classmates about your visits. Take notes so you can tell other people about it later.

	name:	name:	name:
Name of the castle			
Where it is			
Other information: (How old? How big? Who lives or lived there? Is it scary? …)			
What you liked there			
What you didn't like there			

Christmas dinner with Lord and Lady Saye

Imagine you could go to Christmas dinner with Lord and Lady Saye. You can make up other guests. What are they talking about? Write it down.

_____
_____
_____
_____
_____
_____
_____
_____
_____
_____
_____

6 Worksheet

B. That's life: A trip to the seaside

Pre-viewing

Let's go to the seaside!

Maya, Josh and Greg want to make a list of what they should take to the seaside, but the words got all scrambled! Can you help them to write their list? The pictures can help you to find the words but there isn't a picture for every word.

- wanschdi
- gab
- trawe
- tansuh
- bilome hnope
- labl
- lovelupr
- pirssc
- glunssssea
- ymeno

While-viewing

What are they doing?

a) *Listen to the film but don't look at it. Where are Maya, Greg and Josh? Cut out the pictures and put them in the right order.*

A B C
D E F

52

b) *Watch the film now and fill in the gaps.*

1. Dad: I came here a lot when I was a _____!

   Maya: Can we _____ along it?

2. Josh: It's the _____ pier in the world!

   Greg: What are we walking for? There's a _____!

   Maya: Because it's more _____ _____!

3. Josh: Let's _____ Adventure Island!

   That looks _____!

4. Maya: I've got some real Southend Rock for my _____ _____.

   Josh: What does this _____?

   Maya: It says Southend Rock all the _____ through!

5. Greg: Come on, Josh. Or you'll be the _____ one in!

   Josh: You two go first – I think I'll take some _____!

6. Maya: Show us the _____ then! Let's have a look!

   Dad: Well, when I was a _____ I always caught lots of _____.

   Greg: Fish and _____? What are we _____ for! Let's go!

Post-viewing

Greg's e-mail to his friend Peter

That evening Greg wrote an e-mail to his friend Peter in Scotland. He wanted to tell him everything about the day at the seaside. Imagine you are Greg! What would you write to Peter?

You can start like this:

Today my dad took Maya, Josh and me on a trip to the seaside. He wanted to catch a lot of fresh fish...

Unit 7
A. Focus on: Typically British

Overview

Sequence	Track	Duration	Characters	Storyline
Studio	Track 37	00:40	Dave, Rani	
A. Focus on: Typically British	Track 38	09:21	Maya, Josh and Greg	Maya, Josh and Greg give an overview of typical things you come across when you go to Britain, like customs, food, languages, games and traditions.

Ziele
- über Unterschiede zwischen Großbritannien und Deutschland sprechen
- das *present progressive* zur Bildbeschreibung verwenden
- Festigung des *future I* auch im Zusammenhang mit *if-clause type I*

Neuer Wortschatz

remote, to change, fried, unfortunately, toast, marmalade, croissant, milkman, to queue, line, to get into, less, stress, kebab, wicket, bonnie, Highland Games, log, to toss the caber, kilt, Welsh, Wales, dragon, Morris Dancer, Morris Dancing, dance, to watch out, electrical, to hand back, laugh, shot, fussy, Hollywood, exactly, mean, Spain, director

Pre-viewing

Typically German – typically British

Spielen Sie pantomimisch eine Tätigkeit vor bzw. zeichnen Sie ein Ding/eine Situation an die Tafel, die als „typisch deutsch" gelten kann. S erraten dies auf Englisch. S nennen weitere für Deutschland typische Dinge. Leiten Sie dann zum Inhalt des Films über.

L *If you visit Britain, some things will be different. This is what Unit 7 of Action UK! is about. But what do you think will be different? Find at least five things. You can use your English book for help. Then mime or draw what you've found in front of the class.*

Schreiben Sie die Überschrift der Videosequenz *Typically British* an die Tafel und lassen Sie S Vermutungen äußern, was sie sehen werden. Lassen Sie S fünf oder mehr Dinge pantomimisch oder zeichnerisch darstellen, die vermutlich in Großbritannien anders sind als in Deutschland.

TIPP
In leistungsschwächeren Gruppen könnten Sie selbst durch Fragen, Pantomime und/oder kleine Zeichnungen an der Tafel helfen, z. B. eine dampfende Tasse Tee, eine Straße mit Linksverkehr, eine Schuluniform oder ein Geldschein.

Lösungsvorschlag zu a)
They speak English. They drive on the left. They have got school uniforms. They often drink tea. They have got games like cricket and rugby. They have got pounds and pence. Before lessons they have got Registration and Assembly. They start school at nine o'clock. They have got great football players like David Beckham. The best pop music comes from Britain.

While-viewing

Worksheet, p. 58

Living in Britain

Verteilen Sie das Aufgabenblatt. In Teil a) dieser Aufgabe kreuzen S während des Sehens oder unmittelbar danach die Gegenstände an, die sie im Film wahrgenommen haben. Im Aufgabenteil b) füllen S die Tabelle aus, indem sie diese Gegenstände den sieben kurzen Szenen zuordnen und passende Überschriften für die Szenen 2–6 finden. S vergleichen die Lösungen mit einem Partner/einer Partnerin und sprechen darüber, was sie in der jeweiligen Szene gesehen haben.

TIPP
Leistungsstärkere S können vergleichende Sätze schreiben, z. B.:
In Britain you can have chips with salt and vinegar. In Germany we eat chips with salt, ketchup or mayonnaise.

> **Lösung zu b)**
> *Individuelle Schülerlösungen*

Right or wrong?

Worksheet, p. 59

Erklären Sie S die Aufgabenstellung. Weisen Sie ausdrücklich darauf hin, dass mehrere Antworten richtig sein können. Spielen Sie dann die Sequenz vollständig vor. S kreuzen während des Sehens die Sätze an, die für die jeweilige Filmszene zutreffend sind. Zeigen Sie die Sequenz erneut. Abschließend wird die Lösung gemeinsam besprochen.

> **Lösung**
> 1. b); 2. a) b); 3. a) c); 4. a) c); 5. a) c); 6. a) c).

Post-viewing

Watch out!

Worksheet, p. 59

In Teil a) sollten S, nachdem sie sich das Bild drei Minuten lang angesehen haben, abwechselnd in Partnerarbeit sagen, was sie aus dem Video wiedererkannt haben. Es empfiehlt sich, S die Gegenstände und Personen umkreisen und nummerieren zu lassen, da sie sie so besser behalten. Ziehen Sie zur Überprüfung eine Folie und lassen Sie die genannten Situationen einkreisen; ergänzen Sie gegebenenfalls die Dinge, die nicht genannt wurden. Weisen Sie S darauf hin, dass die Zeit, in der sie das Bild beschreiben, das *present progressive* ist.

> **TIPP**
> Die schriftliche Fixierung der Lösung könnte in die Hausaufgabe verlegt werden. Da S dieses Alters noch gern ausmalen, könnte das Bild auch farbig gestaltet werden.

> **Lösung zu a)**
> *Two men are wearing kilts. The cars are driving on the left. A milkman is delivering milk. People are queuing at the bus stop. A boy is wearing cricket clothes. Two people are speaking Welsh.*

Im Aufgabenteil b) finden S die Unterschiede zu einer Straßenszene in Deutschland heraus. S formulieren frei. In leistungsschwächeren Gruppen geben Sie bitte einige Satzmuster vor, z.B. *In Germany we don't have/can't see …* oder *There is/are no … in Germany.*

> **TIPP**
> Nachdem zwei bis drei Beispiele von S gefunden worden sind, eignet sich diese Aufgabe auch als Hausaufgabe.

> **Lösungsvorschlag zu b)**
> 1. *In Germany cars don't drive on the left side of the road.*
> 2. *There are no men in kilts in Germany.*
> 3. *People in Germany don't speak Welsh.*
> 4. *We don't watch cricket on TV. We watch football.*
> 5. *We don't have an English breakfast. Most people eat bread and jam.*
> 6. *In Germany there are no milkmen. We buy our milk in a supermarket.*
> 7. *Policemen in Germany wear a different uniform.*
> 8. *People in Germany don't queue at bus stops.*
> 9. *In Germany we pay with euros, not with pounds.*
> 10. *We eat kebabs in Germany, too, but we call them Döner.*

If you go to Britain

Im Anschluss an die Filmsequenz können S die *if-clauses type I* und somit auch *future I* üben. Hierzu können Sie Satzanfänge vorgeben, etwa:
1. *If you go to Britain, you …*
2. *If you want to go by bus, …*
3. *If you visit Scotland, …*
4. *If you want to buy a cinema ticket, …*
5. *If you eat fish and chips, …*

Oder starten Sie mit dem Satzanfang *If you go to Britain, you…* eine Kettenübung.

Action UK! Studio

Overview

Sequence	Track	Duration	Characters	Storyline
Action UK! Studio	Track 39	03:40	Dave, Rani, Maya, Josh, Greg	Rani and Dave are talking about our three kids' report about life in Britain when Maya, Josh and Greg jump into the studio. Rani and Dave interview the reporters about the making of the video and their plans for the summer holidays.

Ziele
- über Urlaubspläne sprechen
- Festigung des *present progressive* mit Zukunftsaspekt

Pre-viewing

Fragen Sie, was wohl Inhalt der letzten Sequenz von *Action UK! 2* sein könnte und sammeln Sie die Vorschläge auf Folie oder an der Tafel. Danach wird in Form einer Abstimmung die Rangfolge der möglichen Inhalte ermittelt.

L a) *This is the last sequence of Action UK! 2. What do you expect to see?*

Für schwächere Gruppen können Sie die Ideen aus der unten stehenden Box auf eine Folie kopieren oder Sie bereiten ein Arbeitsblatt vor, auf dem S ihre Vorschläge ankreuzen können. S wählen die Ideen, die ihnen plausibel erscheinen und stimmen die wahrscheinlichsten Möglichkeiten ab.

> **TIPP**
> Lassen Sie auf dem von Ihnen erstellten Arbeitsblatt so viel Platz, dass S eigene Ideen entwickeln können.

1. The three reporters are talking about what they will show us in Action UK! 3.
2. The three reporters are meeting Rani and Dave in the studio.
3. There is a party with the three reporters and Dave and Rani.
4. Dave and Rani are visiting Greg, Maya and Josh in Greenwich.
5. The three reporters are telling us about their plans for the summer holidays.
6. The three reporters and Tess are winning a prize at the audition with Greg's song.
7. Maya, Josh and Greg are telling Dave and Rani about the making of the video – what they liked and what they didn't like.
8. The three reporters are at a school party at Thomas Tallis.

Lösung
Individuelle Schülerlösungen

L b) *Now let's watch the video and see which of your ideas are right.*

Zeigen Sie als Ergebnissicherung das Video. Rahmen Sie auf einer Folie mit den von Ihnen vorgegebenen Sätzen und den zusätzlichen Ideen der S die Inhalte ein, die im Video vorkommen. Geben Sie folgenden Satzanfang vor:
Number x is correct because…

Lösung
2., 5., 7.

While-viewing

At Broughton Castle

Worksheet, p. 60

Zeigen Sie den Film bis zu der Stelle, wo Josh in der Einspielung aus *Broughton Castle* sagt: *"OK, not here. Come on."* und lassen Sie in Teil a) dieser Übung während des Sehens die richtigen Aussagen ankreuzen. Im b)-Teil der Übung korrigieren S die Satzanfänge vor dem erneuten Sehen des Outtakes und schreiben (mit Bleistift) mögliche Lösungen, so weit sie sie noch wissen, auf. Spielen Sie dann den Film ein weiteres Mal vor. Es ist erlaubt mitzuschreiben. Sie sollten S jedoch darauf aufmerksam machen, dass beim Schreiben Seh- und Hörzeit verloren geht. Im Anschluss daran lesen S ihre Sätze vor oder erhalten das Skript, um ihre Ergebnisse auf Richtigkeit zu überprüfen. Zeigen Sie im c)-Teil der Übung den kurzen Filmausschnitt noch einmal. S schauen aufmerksam zu und achten besonders auf Gestik, Mimik und die situationsbezogene Intonation. Einzelne Schülergruppen spielen abschließend die kurze Szene vor.

> **Lösung**
> a) ☑ 2.; 6.; 8.; 9.; 12.
> b) 1. Josh: I don't like that wall. 3. Tourist: Are you making a film? 4. Tourist: Can I have your autograph? 5. Tourist: So, where are you from? Hollywood? 7. Tourist: So, are you a famous star then? 10. Josh: It's a film for schools. 11. Tourist: Ohh, great!

Holidays

Worksheet, p. 61

In dieser etwas schwierigeren Übung stehen das Hörverstehen und die Zuordnung von Gehörtem zu den abgebildeten Porträtfotos im Vordergrund. Zeigen Sie die abschließende Studioszene und lassen Sie S die zusammen gehörenden Satzhälften miteinander verbinden und den Satz dem jeweiligen Sprecher zuordnen. S sehen den Ausschnitt ein zweites Mal und überprüfen ihre Lösungen.

> **Lösung**
> 1. + d): Rani; 2. + i): Josh; 3. + j): Dave; 4. + g): Rani; 5. + a): Dave; 6. + k): Maya; 7. + c): Greg; 8. + b): Josh; 9. + e): Rani; 10. + f): Greg; 11. + l): Josh; 12. + h): Rani.

Post-viewing

Let's talk about holidays

Worksheet, p. 61

Schreiben Sie das Wort *HOLIDAYS* in Großbuchstaben auf die Mitte einer Folie/der Tafel und bitten Sie S spontan die Gedanken zu äußern, die sie mit diesem Begriff verbinden. Erläutern Sie dann die Arbeitsaufträge. S übertragen den Anfang der *mind map* in ihr Heft oder auf ein großes Blatt Papier und ergänzen sie zuerst in Einzelarbeit, dann im Austausch mit einem Partner/einer Partnerin. Sie können die *mind map* aber auch, vor allem wenn nicht viel Zeit für diese Phase zur Verfügung steht, gemeinsam mit S entwickeln. Abschließend sprechen S in Kleingruppen über die Urlaubspläne für die bevorstehenden Sommerferien.

> **Lösung**
> *Individuelle Schülerlösungen*

The Action UK! holidays chant

Worksheet, p. 61

Der abschließende *Holidays Chant* bietet ein auflockerndes Element zum Abschluss der Arbeit mit dem Film. S lesen den Text, sprechen nach und tragen den *chant* dann einzeln, in Gruppen oder als Klasse vor. Im b)-Teil der Übung schreiben S eigene kleine *chants* zum Thema *Holidays* und bringen sie zu Gehör.

> **TIPP**
> Führen Sie einen „Sängerwettbewerb" in der Klasse durch. Eine Klassenjury kürt den besten *holidays chant*.

7 Worksheet

A. Focus on: Typically British

While-viewing

Living in Britain

a) *Look at this picture. Find 14 things that you see or hear about in the film. While you watch tick ☑ the right things.*

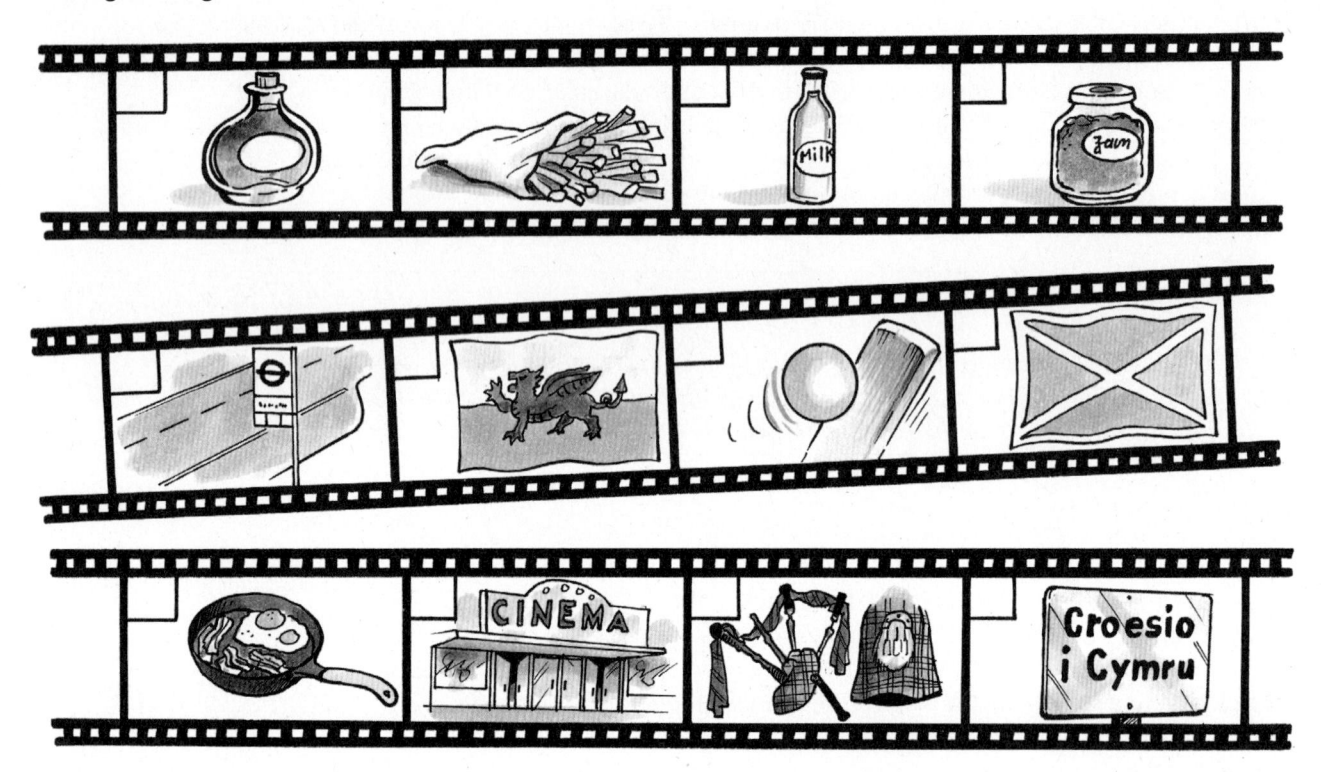

b) *What things go with which scene? Write them down in the list. Add other things that you see in the film. Find a title for scenes 2 – 6. Work with a partner.*

scene 1: English breakfast	scene 2:	scene 3:	scene 4:	scene 5:	scene 6:	scene 7: Morris dancers

Worksheet 7

Right or wrong?

Tick ☑ the right sentence(s). One, two or three sentences can be right.

1

a) ☐ Bacon and egg is Maya's favourite.
b) ☐ Greg drinks milk in his tea.
c) ☐ Josh brings milk to Maya's door.

2

a) ☐ In Britain people always queue.
b) ☐ They queue at bus stops.
d) ☐ But they never queue at the toilet.

3

a) ☐ Greg loves fish and chips.
b) ☐ He eats them with salt and ketchup.
c) ☐ There are many other takeaway foods.

4

a) ☐ Cricket is not easy to play.
b) ☐ It is a Chinese sport.
c) ☐ A game can go on for many days.

5

a) ☐ Many people like the Highland Games.
b) ☐ Boys wear kilts at school.
c) ☐ Men wear kilts for traditional dancing.

6

a) ☐ The Welsh have got their own flag.
b) ☐ There is a horse on it.
c) ☐ They have got their own language, too.

Post-viewing

Watch out!

a) *Look at the picture for three minutes. There are six things in it from the video. Tell your partner about them.*

b) *What would be different in a picture from Germany? Discuss with a partner.*

7 Worksheet

Action UK! Studio

While-viewing

At Broughton Castle

a) *Tick the right sentences.*

1. ☐ Josh: I don't like the castle.
2. ☐ Maya: Oh! You're so fussy, Josh.
3. ☐ Tourist: Are you making a video?
4. ☐ Tourist: Can I take your photo?
5. ☐ Tourist: So, where are you from? London?
6. ☐ Maya: We're from Greenwich.
7. ☐ Tourist: So, are you a famous pop singer then?
8. ☐ Maya: Well, not really famous.
9. ☐ Tourist: When will your film be in the cinema?
10. ☐ Josh: It's a TV film.
11. ☐ Tourist: Ohh, bad!
12. ☐ Josh: OK. Let's go.

b) *Correct the wrong sentences.*

_____
_____
_____
_____
_____
_____

c) *Get together in groups of three. Watch the film again. Then practise and act the dialogue.*

Worksheet 7

Holidays

Who says what? Put the parts of the sentences together. Then draw lines between the pictures and the right sentences.

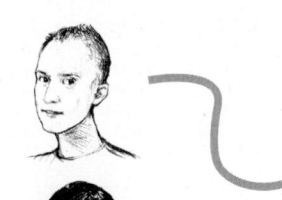

1. And now it's time for the summer
2. Maybe,
3. Are you going away,
4. Sunny Spain!
5. So, what are your plans
6. I'm going to
7. They've got some real cool castles
8. My Mum's taking me to
9. What about you,
10. I'm going to Scotland,
11. Yeah, we're flying to
12. Maybe you'll meet

a) for the summer, guys?
b) Hollywood.
c) with dungeons!
d) holidays for all of us.
e) Maya?
f) camping with my family.
g) Ooh! That sounds fun.
h) a famous Hollywood director!
i) you never know!
j) Josh?
k) Spain.
l) America!

Post-viewing

Let's talk about holidays

a) *Collect all your ideas on holidays in a mind map.*

b) *Present your mind map to a partner. Add new ideas to your mind map.*

c) *Get together in groups of four. Talk about your holiday plans for this summer. Where are you going? How long are you staying there? Who is going with you? What do you want to do there? etc.*

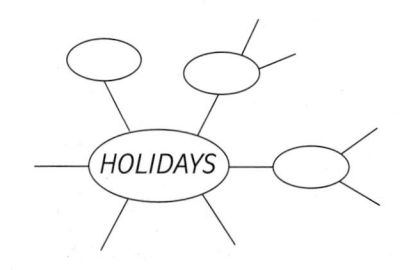

The Action UK! Holidays chant

clap clap Action UK!
clap clap our reporters:
clap clap Josh and Greg
clap clap Maya – they're great!
clap clap What do they want?
clap, clap, clap
Give us an   H   clap clap clap
Give us an   O   clap clap clap
Give us an   L   clap clap clap
Give us an   I   clap clap clap
Give us some   DAYS   clap clap clap
What does it spell? clap clap clap
HOLIDAYS – YEAH!

Lernportfolio

Lernportfolio zu *Action UK! 2*

A So gehe ich mit Filmen um (zum Schuljahresbeginn)

1. Trage ein, wie oft du das in den vergangenen Monaten gemacht hast:

   ✧✧✧ häufig   ✧✧ gelegentlich   ✧ selten   – nie

Fernsehen geschaut		überlegt, wie ein Film gedreht ist	
Spielfilme angesehen		nachgedacht, wo die Kamera steht	
Filme auf Englisch gesehen		beachtet, was die Musik bewirkt	

2. Welche Art von Filmen siehst du vor allem an?

3. Warum gefallen dir bestimmte Filme besser?

B Meine Meinung zu *Action UK! 2* (nach Unit 4)

1. Wen magst du in *Action UK! 2*? Warum? Und wen magst du nicht? Warum nicht?

2. Notiere dir vier Punkte, auf die du besonders achten möchtest, wenn du dir in den nächsten acht Wochen Filme ansiehst.

3. Schreibe vier Dinge auf, die du gerne in *Action UK! 2* sehen würdest, die aber nicht vorhanden sind.

C Das habe ich durch *Action UK! 2* gelernt (nach Unit 7)

1. Notiere vier Aspekte, an die du dich aus *Action UK! 2* erinnerst.

2. Erkläre einem Schüler, der *Action UK! 2* nicht kennt, was man durch den Film alles lernen kann (vier Dinge).

3. Welche Rolle hättest du gerne / nicht gerne in *Action UK! 2* gespielt? Warum? Warum nicht?

Alphabetical word list

A
a long time	ewig	2
	eine lange Zeit	5
a lot	ziemlich oft	3
accident	Unfall	3
Action!	Achtung, Aufnahme!	1
Adventure Island	*Name eines Vergnügungsparks*	6
advert	Werbespot	6
aerobics	Aerobics	5
to be afraid	fürchten	6
air	Luft	2
all over Britain	in ganz Großbritannien	5
all round	um … herum	2
all the way through	ganz durch	6
to allow	erlauben	3
almost	fast	6
along	entlang	6
alright	OK	5
American	amerikanisch	4
anyone	irgendjemand	5
anytime	jederzeit	2
area	Zone	2
argument	Auseinandersetzung	4
arm	Arm	3
armour	Rüstung	6
arms	Waffen	6
around about	ungefähr	2
as	wie	1
at least	mindestens	5
at the front of	vorne	6
Australia	Australien	1
autograph	Autogramm	4

B
bait	Köder	6
to become	werden	4
best	am besten	4
to bet	wetten	6
big wheel	Riesenrad	2
BMX	BMX	1
boat	Boot	2
body	Körper	5
bonnie	schöne	7
brilliant	super, spitze	2
Broughton Castle	*Name eines Schlosses in der Nähe von London*	6
Buckingham Palace	*Haus der Königin in London*	2
building	Gebäude	2
bully	Rabauke	3
bush	Busch	3
busy	ausgefüllt	1

C
to call out	rufen	1
camera	Videokamera	1
cameraman	Kameramann	2
camping	campen	1
can	Dose	5
Canary Wharf Tower	*Bürogebäude in London*	2
canteen	Kantine	5
carrot	Karotte	5
to catch, caught	fangen, fing	6
to change	wechseln	7
cheap	billig	3
cheapest	billigste/r/s	2
to check	herausfinden	1
cheeseburger	Cheeseburger	5
chef	Koch/Köchin	5
to chop	schneiden	5
Christmas	Weihnachten	6
Christmas pudding	Plumpudding	6
class	Kurs	5
classical	Klassik *(Musikrichtung)*	4
clotted cream	cremige Sahne	6
coat	Mantel	3
coke	Cola	5
colony	Kolonie	5
cos	weil	2
cornflake	Cornflake	6
to cost	kosten	2
crazy	verrückt	1
cream tea	*englischer 'Cream Tea'*	6
croissant	Croissant	7
to cut in half	halbieren	6
Cut!	Schnitt!	1

D
dance	Tanz	7
dangerous	gefährlich	1
delicious	lecker	5
difference	Unterschied	4
director	Regisseur	7
dish	Gericht	5
dot	Punkt	2
dragon	Drache	7
drummer	Schlagzeuger/in	4

E
each	pro Person; jede/jeder/jedes	2
earring	Ohrring	3
electrical	elektrisch	7
Elvis	Elvis Presley	4
energy	Kraft	5
even if	selbst wenn	4

Glossar

exactly	genau	7
except	außer	4
to exercise	bewegen	5
to expect	erwarten	6

F

far	weit	2
fashion	Mode	3
to feel ill	schlecht gehen	5
to film	filmen	2
fine	OK	6
fishing	Angeln	2
fitness	Fitness	5
fizzy	mit Kohlensäure	5
flight	Flug	2
flower	Blume	6
freezing	eiskalt	6
fried	gebraten	7
fun park	Fun Park	6
further	weiter	6
fussy	kleinlich	7

G

gardening	Gartenarbeit	2
garlic	Knoblauch	5
to get into	reinkommen	7
Get on with it!	Fang endlich an!	5
to get up to	machen	2
to give in	aufgeben	5
to give it a try	ausprobieren	4
glasses	Brille	2
glove	Handschuh	1
to go around	drehen	2
to go shopping	einkaufen gehen	2
Gosh!	Mensch!	2
Great Hall	Speisesaal	6
guide book	Reiseführer	2
guitarist	Gitarrist/in	4

H

hair	Haar	2
to hand back	zurückgeben	7
to have a look	anschauen	2
Have fun!	Viel Spaß!	6
health	Gesundheit	5
heavy	schwer	6
heavy metal	Heavy Metal (Musikrichtung)	4
helmet	Helm	1
Help yourself.	Bedien dich.	5
Highland Games	Hochland Spiele	7
hip hop	Hip Hop (Musikrichtung)	4
to hit	schlagen	5
Hollywood	Hollywood	7
hood	Kapuze	3
horrible	gemein	3
hot	scharf	5
Houses of Parliament	englisches Parlamentsgebäude	2
human body	menschlicher Körper	5
to hurt	weh tun	3

I

in front of	vor	1

J

jam	Marmelade	6
jazz dance	Jazz (Musikrichtung)	5
jealous	eifersüchtig	3
Jemma	weibl. Vorname	3
to joke	Witze machen	1
jumble sale	Flohmarkt	2
Just a minute.	Warte mal!	1

K

kebab	Kebap	7
Kellogs	Firmenname	6
ketchup	Ketschup	1
keyboard	Keyboard	4
kilometre	Kilometer	2
kilt	Schottenrock	7
king	König	4
knee pad	Knieschoner	1

L

ladies' fingers	Okra	5
lady	Dame	5
Lady	Lady	6
laugh	Spaß	7
lead singer	Sänger/in	4
to leave	übrig lassen	6
Leave me alone.	Lass mich in Ruhe.	3
less	weniger	7
to let	erlauben	6
Let's get on with it.	Lass/t uns weitermachen.	2
Like what?	Zum Beispiel?	2
line	Schlange	7
litre	Liter	5
log	Stamm	7
longest	längste	6
to look	aussehen	4
to look after	aufpassen	6
Lord	Herr	6
love	Schatz	3
low	niedrig	1
lucky things	Glückspilze	6

M

to make sure	aufpassen	1
market	Markt	3
marmalade	Orangenmarmelade	7
mate	Freund/in	4
mean	gemein	7
meat	Fleisch	5
mile	Meile	2
milkman	Milchmann	7
mine	meine/meiner/meins	2
Miss	Anrede für eine Lehrerin	1

Glossar

Morris Dancer	Morris-Tänzer	7
Morris Dancing	Morris-Tanz	7
to move	bewegen	2
muffin	Muffin	5
myself	mich, mir	3

N
necklace	Halskette	3
needn't worry	keine Sorgen machen	3
Nelson's Column	*Nelson Säule*	2
news	Nachrichten	2
next time	nächstes Mal	1
noisy	laut	4
to not feel so good	nicht so gut gehen	5
notebook	Notizbuch	1
nothing	nichts	3

O
on your marks … get set … go	auf die Plätze … fertig … los	5
onion	Zwiebel	5
open air	im Freien	4
or else	sonst	3
others	andere/anderen	4
ourselves	uns	4
over to you	jetzt zu dir	1
owner	Besitzer/in	6

P
pardon me	Entschuldigung!	5
to pass	bestehen	4
PE kit	Sportzeug	1
personality	Persönlichkeit	4
pier	Landesteg	6
piercing	Piercing	3
plane	Flugzeug	2
playing field	Sportplatz	1
pocket money	Taschengeld	2
poor	arm	1
popstar	Popstar	2
Post Office Tower	*Bürogebäude in London*	2
powder	Pulver	5
to prefer	bevorzugen	4
pretty	ziemlich	2
private	privat	4
punk	Punk *(Musikrichtung)*	4

Q
queen	Königin	2
to queue	Schlange stehen	7

R
to read out	vorlesen	1
receipt	Quittung	6
reggae	Reggae *(Musikrichtung)*	4
Registration	Registrierung *(Schulfach)*	1
remote	ferngesteuert	7
report	Bericht	1
reporter	Reporter/in	1
rest	Pause	5
ride	Fahrgeschäft	6
roast	gebraten	6
rock	Rock *(Musikrichtung)*	4
	Lutschstange	6
rock 'n' roll	Rock-'n'-Roll *(Musikrichtung)*	4
to roll	laufen	6
Royal Festival Hall	*Konzerthalle in London*	2
rucksack	Rucksack	1
rugby	Rugby	1
to run off	abhauen	4

S
sale	Schlussverkauf	3
salt	Salz	5
salted	gesalzen	5
same	derselbe	1
same	dieselbe	3
it says	da steht	2
Saye	*Familienname*	6
at the seaside	am Meer	6
see you	bis dann	2
series	Sendefolge	1
serious	ernst	5
Serpentine Lake	*See im Hyde Park*	2
Shakespeare in Love	*Filmtitel*	6
shorts	Shorts	3
shot	Szene	7
should	sollte/sollten	3
show	Sendung	3
single	einzige/r/s	6
sleep	Schlaf	2
sleepover	Übernachtung	2
slow	langsam	2
slow down	langsamer werden	2
slowly	langsam	2
to smell	riechen	6
smokey bacon	geräucherter Bauchspeck	5
sneaker	Turnschuh	3
something else	etwas anderes	5
sometime	irgendwann	2
soon	gleich	1
to sound	anhören	1
Southend	*Badeort in England*	6
Spain	Spanien	7
St Paul's Cathedral	*Londoner Dom*	2
to stand by	aufpassen	5
star	Star	1
still	ohne Kohlensäure	5
strawberry	Erdbeere	6
stress	Stress	7
string	Saite	2
to string	Saiten aufziehen	2
studio	Studio	1
stupid	dumm	4
surprised	überrascht	2
sword	Schwert	6

65

Glossar

T

to take a look	etw. anschauen	1
to take photographs	fotografieren	4
tall	hoch	2
tallest	höchste	2
tattoo	Tattoo	3
tea room	Café	6
texting	SMS schicken	3
thick	dick	6
tiring	anstrengend	5
toast	Toast	7
to toss the caber	Stammwerfen	7
totally	völlig	3
tour	Tour	4
Tower Bridge	*Brücke über die Themse*	2
track	Track	4
traditional	traditionell	6
Trafalgar Square	*Platz in London*	2
turkey	Pute	6

U

unfortunately	leider	7
until	bis	1
upset	sauer	3

V

vegetarian	Vegatarier/in	5
village	Dorf	5
vinegar	Essig	5

W

Wales	Wales	7
walled garden	ummauerter Garten	6
to watch out	aufpassen	7
Welsh	walisisch	7
What are … up to?	Was machen …?	2
What else happened?	Was ist sonst noch passiert?	1
What on earth …?	Was in aller Welt …?	3
whatever	was auch immer	5
wicked	geil	3
wicket	Dreistab	7

Y

yet	schon	2
Yikes!	Wah!	6
yummy	lecker	6

Filmskripte

Unit 1

Action UK! Studio
Dave: Hi there!
Rani: Hello!
Dave: I'm Dave!
Rani: And my name is Rani.
Dave: Hi, Rani!
Rani: Hi, Dave! Welcome to Action UK! 2. It's good to be back.
Dave: This is our second series of programmes about Britain. Rani and I are here in the studio.
Rani: And our three reporters Maya, Josh and Greg are back with us, too. They're in Greenwich. Today is their first day back at Thomas Tallis School after the holidays.
Dave: Let's take a look!

A. Focus on: Back to school

Maya: Stop that, Greg! You and your crazy tricks! Josh is ready. We must start our report now! School starts soon!
Greg: Oh, sorry! How long is it until school starts?
Maya: Ten minutes. It's half past eight.
Josh: OK, you two. Are you ready? Come and stand here in front of the camera. Here we are at Thomas Tallis School. Our report for you today is about the first day of the new school year. And here are our reporters to tell you about it.
Maya: Hi, everyone! Great to see you again! Hi, Josh! I'm Maya and I'm your star reporter!
Greg: No, you're not.
Maya: OK, OK, I'm only joking! Here we are back at Thomas Tallis School after the summer holidays. I hope we have some cool new teachers this year!
Josh: Great! Over to you, Greg!
Greg: Hello! My name's Greg and I'm in the same class as Maya and Josh. On the first day back we get all our new books from our teachers. So I've got this cool new bag!
Maya: But you've still got your old uniform!
Greg: It's OK.
Maya: It's too small!
Teacher: Hi, you three – are you making another film?
Josh: Yes, Miss! We're doing a report about the first day back at school.
Teacher: Great! But make sure you're not late for your lessons!
Maya: OK!
Teacher: OK, bye!
Maya: Bye!
Josh: OK, let's go to Registration.
Maya: We have Registration every morning. The teacher calls out all the names to check who is at school.
Greg: Sometimes we go to Assembly in the hall. Different year groups have Assembly on different days. This is the Year 10 assembly. After Assembly we go to our first lesson.
Josh: On our first day back at school, we get our new exercise books from our teachers.
Maya: At Thomas Tallis we have lessons from 8:50 to 10:50, then we have break. Break is for twenty minutes. We can go to the playground or to the playing field.
Greg: Or have a snack.
Maya: Or we can buy things from the school shop. Mrs Shields works here. We can buy our uniform and PE kit here, and pencils and notebooks, too.
Greg: After break there are more lessons until lunchtime. These pupils are doing English. These pupils are doing Science.
Josh: At lunchtime we can buy food and eat it in the cafeteria. The food here is very good for you!
Greg: After lunch there are more lessons! These pupils are doing Art. These are doing PE.
Maya: OK, Josh. And action! So Josh – how was the first day back at school for you this year? What did you like about it and what wasn't so good?
Josh: Well, this morning we had English. This year we've got Mrs Davies – she's one of my favourite teachers.
Greg: Yeah – she doesn't give much homework!
Josh: We wrote stories about the summer holidays and read them out.
Greg: Tim Brown's was really funny – he went camping in Scotland and it rained every day.
Maya: That doesn't sound very funny to me! What else happened?
Josh: Well, Greg got ketchup on his sweatshirt at lunchtime. Now he really needs a new one!
Greg: Ha! Ha! Ha! And Josh's mobile rang in the history lesson – so he's got extra homework tonight!
Josh: Thanks, Greg.
Maya: OK, great. Are there any new people this year?
Josh: Yes – there's a new boy in our class. He's from Australia! He came here in August.
Greg: And there's a new PE teacher: He's a really good rugby player – he played for England when he was at school!
Maya: OK, thanks. And cut! Come on Josh – the Samba Band starts in a minute.
Greg: And action!
Maya: After school there are lots of clubs that pupils can go to. In here, the Samba Band is practising. We can't do our report in there because it's too difficult to hear us when the band is playing!
Josh: It's great music to dance to.
Maya: Hey – cool! Come on, let's go in! And action!
Josh: So that's the end of a very busy day! It's 4:30 and we're going home to have some tea, do some homework and maybe watch some TV.
Greg: And I'm going to practise on my BMX bike. BMX Club starts next week and I want to be good!
Josh: What about our Maths homework, Greg?
Greg: Err – where's my planner? We don't have any Maths homework! Great! Bye!
Maya: And cut!
Josh: Bye!

Action UK! Studio
Dave: What a busy day!
Rani: What a lot of different subjects!
Dave: Yes. And what a cool school!
Rani: I'd love to go to the Samba Club! What about you?
Dave: Well, I'd like to see Greg on his BMX – it sounds great fun.
Rani: Well – maybe you can! Let's take a look.

B. That's life: BMXing

Greg: Oh hello Maya! … You want to what? … You want to come to the BMX Club. Are you sure? … Yeah … well … OK. A bike? Well – you do need a bike … Yeah – you can have a go on my old bike. … OK then. Now? Oh, OK then. Let's meet

Skripte

	at my house in 10 minutes. ... Right. ... See you then. Bye Maya!
Maya:	Hi, Greg!
Greg:	Hi, Maya!
Stacey:	Hi, Greg! Maya – why do you want to go to the BMX Club? Is it because that new boy in your class wants to go?
Maya:	No – Stacey. My little sister goes everywhere with me.
Greg:	Oh ... right. ... Well – here's the bike, Maya.
Stacey:	Wow! Your new bike's fantastic. I'm sure you can do really good tricks on it. Can you show me some, Greg, pleeease?! I'd love to see some.
Greg:	Err ... OK, Maya?
Maya:	Go on then, Greg – show us what you can do!
Greg:	Thanks. Do you want a go now, Maya?
Maya:	Yeah!
Greg:	Well, here's a helmet for you and you can borrow my gloves and knee pads.
Maya:	Oh, come on, Greg. I don't need those. I'll be really careful!
Greg:	Uh-uh, Maya! You can't be too careful. Tricks aren't easy. And it can be dangerous.
Maya:	OK then. Stacey, take the rucksack, please. Sit over there.
Greg:	It's like a normal bike really. OK, let's go.
Maya:	Oh, I can't sit on that, Greg – it's too low!
Greg:	OK, I'll have a look at it. I think that's OK now.
Maya:	Yeah, that's better. Can you teach me a trick now?
Greg:	Yeah, sure. Let's just go up the road and back for now. Hey, where's my bike?
Maya:	Just a minute, Greg, I think I know where your bike is. Sta-cey! Stacey! Very funny, Stacey – I don't think! Here's your bike, Greg. Now Stacey, say sorry to Greg.
Stacey:	Sorry, Greg.
Greg:	I'm glad I haven't got a little sister!
Maya:	And now I've got a good idea. You can go and buy Greg and me an ice-cream. And we can practise on the bikes. And I don't think you need those crisps. Hungry, Greg?

Action UK! Studio

Dave:	Poor Greg!
Rani:	Ah – that Stacey!
Dave:	Well, that's the end of the first day back at Thomas Tallis!
Rani:	And that's all from Action UK! for today! See you next time!
Dave:	Yep, see you next time!
Rani/Dave:	Bye!

Try it out!
Maya speaking to camera.
– Hi everyone! Great to see you again!
Maya speaking to Stacey.
– Now Stacey, say sorry to Greg.
Sorry, Greg.
Maya speaking to Josh.
– How was the first day back at school for you this year? What did you like about it and what wasn't so good?
Josh speaking to Maya.
– We wrote stories about the summer holidays and read them out.

Unit 2

Action UK! Studio

Dave:	Hello everybody and welcome back to Action UK!
Rani:	I'm Rani!
Dave:	And I'm Dave. What have we got today, Rani?
Rani:	Today we've got a report about what young people like to do at the weekends.
Dave:	What do you like to do at the weekends, Rani?
Rani:	I like to see my friends! Oh, and I like gardening. What about you, Dave? What do you do at the weekends?
Dave:	Me? I like sport and I go fishing! Would you like to see a photo?
Rani:	Thanks, Dave, but we haven't got time for that now. Let's see what Josh, Maya and Greg have got for us today.
Dave:	Great!

A. Focus on: The weekend

Greg:	Right, let's get on with it. I've got football in an hour. And action!
Josh:	Hello! We've got a great report for you today about what young people do at the weekends.
Maya:	Yes, and you can see what we did last weekend, too!
Josh:	How was your weekend?
Girl 1:	Mine was cool. I played computer games with my best friend.
Josh:	How many computer games have you got?
Girl 1:	Around about ten.
Maya:	Hi! How was your weekend?
Girl 2:	It was really good. It was my birthday, I had a party!
Maya:	Cool! And how many people came?
Girl 2:	About 20!
Greg:	Hi, and how was your weekend?
Girl 3:	It was boring.
Maya:	What did you do at the weekend?
Boy 1:	Not much, just watched TV.
Maya:	How much TV did you watch?
Boy 1:	About five hours on Saturday and six hours on Sunday!
Greg:	Hi! What did you do at the weekend?
Boy 2:	I went shopping and bought three new CDs!
Greg:	Three? How much pocket money do you get?
Boy 2:	Ten pound a week!
Greg:	What do you think's more interesting – playing computer games or watching TV?
Girl 4:	Um ... playing computer games are more interesting. Watching TV is boring!
Josh:	Where's the best place to buy CDs?
Boy 3:	Um ... CDs? They're cheapest at HMV.
Maya:	What do you want to do at the weekend?
Girl 5:	Well, I like to stay home and watch DVDs with my friends.
Maya:	Why don't you go to the cinema?
Girl 5:	Well, cos it's cheaper to watch DVDs!
Maya:	Now here are three films about what we did at the weekend!
Josh:	First of all, here's Greg's. I was the cameraman – I'm surprised I can still hear anything.
Greg:	On Saturday I went to a music shop. I bought a song book and some strings for my cool new guitar.
Josh:	It took him a long time to string his guitar!
Greg:	On Sunday I practised some songs from my new book. And then I had an idea for a new song.
Dad:	Greg! Hey, that sounds pretty good.
Greg:	My dad liked my song. But he looked silly playing an air guitar!
Maya:	Wow, Greg – that was great! Can you play your new song for us sometime?
Greg:	Sure! Anytime!
Josh:	Not now, Greg, we need to watch Maya's report.
Maya:	On Saturday night I had a

68

sleepover at my house. Two of my friends from school stayed over. Emma did my hair – what do you think? Later we made a poster for the school 'Popstars' competition. We didn't go to sleep until three in the morning. So we didn't get much sleep! On Sunday we were very tired.

Josh: What is there to talk about until three in the morning?
Maya: Lots of different things!
Greg: Like what?
Maya: I'm not telling you! Let's have a look at what Josh got up to!
Greg: Yeah – we went all round London to film him!
Josh: Last weekend I went to find some places for my new film about London. First I went to Hyde Park. Look, the Serpentine Lake. Then I went to Buckingham Palace. And the Queen was in! There were lots of tourists there! After that I went to Trafalgar Square. It was very busy. That's Nelson's Column. I also went to Tower Bridge, but it didn't open! And here I am filming the Houses of Parliament across the River Thames. Look there's Big Ben.
Maya: Gosh, Josh – you went to a lot of different places!
Greg: Yeah – we did! It took hours. Can I go now? I've got football!
Maya: OK. Go on then. See you.
Josh: Byee!

Action UK! Studio
Dave: Poor Greg! I hope he isn't late for football! But that was interesting, wasn't it?
Rani: Yes, it was.
Dave: So, what are our reporters up to this weekend?
Rani: I think they're doing a school project.
Dave: Well, let's see.

B.   That's Life: The London Eye
Maya: Wow, look at that!
Greg: And look at this!
Josh: OK, slow down. Let me see.
Greg: Look at that about the London Dungeon.
Maya: Sorry. But our project's on the London Eye!
Josh: Right, … www – dot – londoneye – dot – com. Here it is. OK. What have they got?
Greg: Cor, wow! It says you can take a 'flight'. You can go in a plane!
Maya: Don't be silly, Greg. It's not a real flight. The London Eye is a big wheel, like a big bike wheel.
Greg: Well, let's see how much it costs, … errr £6.50 each. That's too expensive for me.
Maya: For me, too. I only get three pounds pocket money a week!
Josh: Yeah! I'll be back in a minute. What do you want to hear first – the good news or the bad news?
Maya/Greg: Bad!/Good!
Maya: Good.
Josh: The good news is: My mum's calling the London Eye. She's buying us tickets for next weekend!
Maya/Greg: Great!/Cool!
Greg: OK – what's the bad news then?
Josh: The bad news is: There's a jumble sale soon and my mum wants us to collect old clothes with her on Saturday.
Greg/Maya: Sure!/No problem.
Josh: Oh, OK.
Greg: OK, Josh. You've got the map. Where are we?
Maya: Over there, Greg, is the Royal Festival Hall. They have lots of concerts there. Everybody knows that!
Greg: Well, I didn't! But it looks great for skateboarding!
Josh: You can't skateboard here! It's a tourist area. You can see all of this from the London Eye.
Maya: Can you see Greenwich?
Josh: I don't know. Let's go and find out!
Greg: Cor – wow, it's so tall.
Josh: Yes, it's 130 metres high – one of the tallest things in London.
Greg: The tallest building in London is Canary Wharf Tower – that's 235 metres high.
Maya: Wow! How far can we see from the top of the London Eye?
Josh: It says here that you can see for 40 kilometres.
Maya: Can we see Greenwich?
Josh: I don't know! Wait and see!
Greg: How fast does it go? It's not moving. It's going really slow! Can't it go any faster?
Josh: Well, it moves very slowly. In a year it goes around 8,000 times.
Maya: How many capsules are there?
Greg: I don't know, they're moving too fast!
Josh: It says here there are 32 capsules and they can take 25 people in each one.
Maya: And that's 15,000 people a day!
Greg: Wow – that was quick, Maya!
Maya: Yeah, I know! I just read it in Josh's guide book! Look, there's The Houses of Parliament!
Josh: Oh, and look over there: Buckingham Palace!
Greg: Look at the boats on the river. They're so small! You can see the River Thames for miles!
Maya: Can you see Greenwich?
Josh: Try looking! Or do you need glasses, Maya!
Maya: Oh, and there's St Paul's Cathedral. Look!
Greg: Is it time for lunch yet? I'm hungry!
Maya: Can't you wait? We can have lunch after the flight.
Greg: But those people are having lunch in their capsule.
Maya: Oh, yes – I think they're having a party!
Josh: Hey, you two! We're here to look at London. We can eat our lunch later!
Maya: That was brilliant. Let's have lunch here.
Greg: OK.
Maya: Greg, where are all the sandwiches?
Greg: Errr, sandwiches? Maybe Josh has got some?
Josh: Greg! Where's all the food?
Greg: Well, I was really hungry!
Maya: Great, Greg, thanks! If we're quick we can get the next bus back into Greenwich and go to my house and have a pizza. Mum bought some for us all yesterday.
Greg: Great! I love pizza!

Action UK! Studio
Rani: Wow, I'd love to go on the London Eye!
Dave: Yes! Me, too. You can see so many famous things – Big Ben, St Paul's, the Post Office Tower!
Rani: Well, that's all for now.
Dave: See you next time!
Rani/Dave: Bye!

Try it out!
Greg speaking to girl.
– Hi and how was your weekend?
Maya speaking to boy.
– What did you do at the weekend?
Josh speaking to girl.
– How many computer games have you got?
Greg speaking to boy.
– How much pocket money do you get?
Greg speaking to girl.
– What do you think's more interesting – playing computer games or watching TV?
Josh speaking to boy.
– Where's the best place to buy CDs?

Unit 3

Action UK! Studio

Dave: Hi, and welcome to another Action UK! show.
Rani: Hi there!
Dave: Well, I like wearing them – I'm starting a new fashion.
Rani: You, Dave? That's not really you, is it?
Dave: Oh, yes, it is me, Rani. It's the new me.
Rani: Hmmm. What's in fashion in your country? Do you know what kids in Britain like wearing?
Dave: Let's watch the report!

A. Focus on: Fashion

Maya: Hi! Today we're talking about fashion in Britain! What's 'in' in Britain? Well, I don't really follow fashion. I usually buy jeans and with them, I usually wear a nice T-shirt, because T-shirts are always in fashion, too!
Greg: You don't follow fashion, Maya? So, why did you go in that shop?
Maya: Oh, yes! To go with my jeans and T-shirt I bought this lovely bag!
Greg: Not another bag, Maya! How many bags do you need?
Maya: You can never have too many bags, Greg!
Greg: YOU can never have too many bags you mean! OK! So tell us what boys here are wearing today.
Maya: Oh yes. Well, what about boys? What do boys like to wear? Here comes Josh – I think he knows more about that than me. Josh?
Josh: Hi, Maya!
Maya: What on earth are you wearing? They're not the right clothes at all!
Josh: Only joking, Maya!
Maya: You had me worried for a minute there!
Greg: OK! Cut! Cool coat, Josh! OK, Maya you take over, over there.
Maya: And action!
Josh: Greg and I wear totally different things, don't we?
Greg: Like Josh never wears shorts.
Josh: And Greg wears shorts a lot. And I spend my pocket money on cool things like these shoes. Wicked, aren't they? And Greg, well … he's happy in his sneakers, isn't he?
Greg: And look at our hair. It's very different, isn't it?
Dave: Today we've got a great show for you. All about what we like to wear.
Rani: Dave, you're wearing earrings!
Josh: I like my hair short.
Greg: And I like my hair long!
Josh: But we both like wearing caps!
Greg: And hats.
Josh: You needn't like all the same things to be good friends. And we're good friends, aren't we?
Greg: Well, yeah.
Maya: OK. Thanks you two! And cut! Now let's go and ask some other kids what they like to wear!
Greg: And action!
Maya: What kind of shoes do you like to wear?
Boy 1: I like trainers like these.
Maya: How much do they cost?
Boy 1: They are very expensive!
Maya: Thank you!
Josh: What kind of clothes do you like to wear?
Boy 2: I like sweatshirts with a hood.
Josh: Wicked!
Maya: Do you follow fashion?
Boy 2: No, not really.
Maya: Thanks.
Greg: Cut!
Maya: What sort of clothes do you like to wear?
Girl 1: Well, I really like skirts and jeans but anything really.
Maya: Who buys them for you?
Girl 1: I buy most of my stuff, but my mum and dad can buy them sometimes.
Maya: I like your necklace. Where did you get it from?
Girl 1: I bought it from the market.
Maya: OK. Thank you.
Josh: And action!
Maya: I really like your T-shirt. Where did you buy it?
Girl 2: I bought it at Top Scene – in the sale! It only cost £2!
Maya: That's really cheap! Do you follow fashion?
Girl 2: Well, I try to. I spend most of my pocket money on clothes!
Maya: Thank you! I like your earrings! Have you got any other piercings?
Girl 3: No! I wanted another piercing but my parents said no. I'm only allowed earrings!
Maya: What about you: Have you got any earrings or tattoos?
Girl 4: No – I don't like piercings or tattoos!
Maya: Thanks! Do you follow fashion?
Josh: What do you and your friends wear – at school and at home?
Dave: Yeah, cool, aren't they?
Rani: Well, they're very nice but I didn't know you liked wearing earrings like that, Dave.

Action UK! Studio

Dave: Do you follow fashion, Rani?
Rani: Follow fashion? Me? Dave, if there's one thing you should know it's this: Fashion follows me!
Dave: Errr, OK!
Rani: Let's go to Maya's flat where her little sister Stacey is upset about something.
Dave: What's she upset about? Did her family forget her birthday? No, I know: Maya's always first in the bathroom in the mornings? No?
Rani: Uh uh. Let's have a look.

B. That's Life: Friends?

Mum: What's that, Stacey?
Stacey: What?
Mum: There's a red scratch on your arm! Here, let me have a look.
Stacey: It's nothing. Leave me alone.
Mum: Let me see. It's a scratch! And it looks very red. What happened, Stacey?
Stacey: It's just a scratch, OK? Leave me alone, can't you?
Dad: Oh, come on, Stacey, love. Don't talk to your mum like that. Now what happened? How did you get that scratch?
Maya: Yeah, did it happen at school, Stacey?
Stacey: I told you, it was an accident, OK!
Maya: It wasn't an accident, was it, Stacey? What happened? You can tell me. I'm your sister.
Stacey: It was Jemma! She's being horrible to me! In PE, she made fun of my trainers and said they were silly. She said they're for little girls, babies! And then she threw them behind a bush.
Maya: What did you do then?
Stacey: I got them, but I scratched my arm on the bush. Then I went over to sit with my friends to talk to them.
Maya: Good! That was the right thing to do! That Jemma's a bully! Your new trainers are cool. She's just jealous. I'm sure she really wants a pair just like yours.
Stacey: She was my best friend! I'm not wearing those again!
Maya: You must wear them, Stacey! You can't let that bully, Jemma, win!

Stacey: But I don't want her to laugh at me again.
Maya: Hmmm. You needn't worry.
Stacey: W-what are you doing?
Maya: I'm sending Jemma a message!
Stacey: A message? What are you texting?
Maya: Leave … my … little sister … alone. … Or else …!
Stacey: No – don't do that! Thanks, Maya. But I must talk to Jemma myself. Hiya!
Mum: Hi! How was school?
Stace: Cool!
Maya: So, Stacey! Did you wear your new trainers today?
Stacey: Of course.
Maya: And did you see that big bully Jemma?
Stacey: Jemma? Oh yeah! She's OK really! We're friends again! And do you know what? She's got some new trainers just like mine!

Action UK! Studio
Rani: Aw! Stacey's happy again. But best friends can be difficult!
Dave: It hurts when your friends say horrible things about the things you like to wear.
Rani: Eh? Oh! No, no … look I'm sorry Dave, but I like your earrings very much, they're really … you!
Dave: Thanks, Rani. It was just a joke. Well, that's all we've got time for.
Rani: See you next time.
Dave/Rani: Bye!

Try it out!
Maya talking to camera.
– I usually buy jeans … and with them, I usually wear a nice T-shirt, because T-shirts are always in fashion, too!
Greg and Maya talking.
– How many bags do you need? You can never have too many bags, Greg!
Maya and girl talking.
– I really like your T-shirt, where did you buy it?
I bought it at Top Scene, in the sale. It only cost two pounds.
– That's really cheap!
Maya and girl talking.
– Do you follow fashion?
Well … I try to, I spend most of my pocket money on clothes.

Unit 4

Action UK! Studio
Rani: Hi, Dave!
Dave: Hi, Rani! How are you?
Rani: Great! Today we're talking about the kind of music people like.
Dave: I like rock and heavy metal.
Rani: Oh, I don't! I think pop and rap music are better.
Dave: What kind of music do you like?
Rani: Do you know what kind of music British kids listen to? Well, our reporters wanted to find out for you.
Dave: Great! Let's have a look.

A. Focus on: Music
Greg: And … ahem … and … action!
Maya: Hi! Most young people like music. But they all like different kinds of music.
Josh: So we made our own CD with different tracks.
Maya: In Britain lots of kids like pop music.
Josh: Others, like me, think that reggae is better. Listen to this. Now that's what I call music!
Maya: Thanks, Josh. Some people prefer rap.
Josh: And disco music.
Greg: Don't forget heavy metal bands!
Josh: And some of my friends like classical music.
Maya: Thanks, you two. I like girl groups and boy bands because their music's usually really good to dance to.
Josh: Some old people like Rock 'n' Roll singers, like Elvis.
Greg: Yeah, Elvis! 'The King of Rock 'n' Roll'.
Josh: No, no, no, Greg! Greg – what are you doing?
Greg: Sorry. I'm still filming … Go on then!
Josh: Most singers and bands in this country are British or American.
Maya: Here in Britain there are lots of TV shows like 'Popstars' where the winners can make a CD and become famous – even if it's only for a week or two. I'd like to do that!
Josh: It's not easy to be a famous music star. You go on tour all the time, there are always new songs to learn, you have no private life because your fans are always asking for your autograph.
Maya: And they're always taking photographs of you!
Greg: Autographs? Photos? No, thanks!
Maya: As you can see, we all like different kinds of music. Josh likes reggae and hip hop.
Josh: And classical music. And Maya likes girl groups, boy bands and wants to become a popstar.
Greg: Hey, what about me?
Josh: Oh sorry, Greg. And Greg likes heavy metal, of course!
Maya: Now you know what we like – let's go and find out what other young people like listening to.
Greg: OK … cut! Hi! Excuse me!
Boy 1: Yeah?
Greg: What kind of music do you like to listen to?
Boy 1: Rock music.
Greg: Cool!
Boy 1: D'you want to listen?
Greg: Yeah. Oh, that's cool!
Maya: Where do you get your music from?
Boy 1: On the market!
Greg: Me, too! And do you go to concerts?
Boy 1: Sometimes.
Greg: Cool!
Maya: Thank you.
Josh: Action!
Maya: So what kind of music do you like to listen to?
Girl 1: Emm, I like punk best.
Greg: Where do you get your music from?
Girl 1: I buy CDs or I get them from my friends.
Maya: And do you go to concerts?
Girl 1: Yeah, I went to an open air concert last year with my mates! That was cool!
Greg: Cool!
Maya: Thanks.
Greg: What kind of music do you like to listen to?
Girl 2: Erm, I like all kinds really, but I don't like heavy metal, it's too noisy!
Maya: Where do you get your music? Do you buy CDs in music shops?
Girl 2: No, that's too expensive. I listen to the radio!
Greg: Do you go to concerts?
Girl 2: No, that's too expensive, too! But I like to watch music videos on TV.
Maya: Thanks! So what kind of music do you like to listen to?

Boy 2: I like hip hop and reggae!
Maya: What's the difference?
Boy 2: Well, hip hop is like reggae – only faster!
Josh: And where do you get your music?
Boy 2: I buy CDs and I download things off the Internet.
Maya: Do you go to concerts?
Boy 2: No! I don't get enough pocket money.
Josh: Thanks.
Maya: Thanks.
Greg: What about you?
Maya: Yeah, what kind of music do you like?

Action UK! Studio
Dave: What an interesting report!
Rani: Yeah, I'd love to be in a band or go on one of those TV shows Maya talked about!
Dave: Well, it's not all fun and games being in a band, you know, Rani. Sometimes the people in the band have arguments.
Rani: Arguments?
Dave: Yes! You know, problems. The keyboard player thinks the guitarist is always late and the lead singer always thinks the drummer is too loud! All those different personalities. Have a look.

B. That's Life: Star Reporters
Josh: Everyone ready? A-one, a-two, a-one, two, three, four. You didn't learn the song, did you, Maya?
Maya: I only had last night to learn it!
Greg: The audition for the concert is in three days!
Maya: Well, you wrote the song, Greg, why don't you sing it!?
Greg: Because you're the singer! How can we pass the audition if the lead singer doesn't know the song?
Josh: OK, OK! Let's try again. A-one, a-two, a-one, two, three, four.
Maya: I can't do this! Why can't we sing Summer Time?
Josh: Because it's better to sing a song we wrote ourselves! And – we haven't got time to practise a new one.
Maya: But I know that one.
All: We don't!
Maya: Well, I don't feel right. We look all wrong.
Greg: What's wrong with our clothes?
Maya: We should wear special clothes, we look like a heavy metal band! And another thing, I don't like our name.
Josh: What's wrong with 'Star Reporters'? You liked it before. You made the poster!
Greg: Yeah, we are reporters – well, except Tess and we want to be stars. Duh, Maya!
Maya: So, you're all against me! I've had enough. I'm leaving! This is stupid!
Josh: Oh! Come on, Maya! Where are you going? What about the audition?
Boys: Wow! Maya! You look great!
Maya: Hi! I'm back. And I've got some things for you.
Greg: Err, what's happening?
Maya: Just give it a try, Greg – put it on!
Josh: Come on, Greg! It's not that bad! Where did you get all this, Maya?
Maya: That's my secret! Come on then. Oh. I'm sorry I ran off like that yesterday. I was upset.
Josh: OK. Well, we do look really cool now! These clothes are much better! But what about our name?
Maya: Oh! 'Star Reporters' is OK really! I was just upset about the song.
Greg: What about the song?
Maya: Oh, I know the song now! It's a good song, too, Greg. But I think we should play it faster. Let's try it!
Greg: OK. Let's give it a try.
Josh: OK. Everyone ready? A-one, a-two, a-one, two, three, four.
Maya: No! Faster! Like this: A-one, a-two, a-one, two, three, four.

Action UK! Studio
Dave: Don't they look great?
Rani: And don't they sound good! What a great song!
Dave: Yeah! It's much better when they play it faster!
Rani: And I see what you mean about problems, Dave.
Dave: Well, that's all we've got time for.
Rani: See you next time!
Dave/Rani: Bye!

Try it out!
Maya speaking to girl.
– What kind of music do you like to listen to?
Greg speaking to girl.
– Where do you get your music from?
Maya speaking to girl.
– Do you go to concerts?

Unit 5

Action UK! Studio
Rani: Welcome to Action UK! And this week our reporters, erm, what's wrong, Dave?
Dave: Well, I went to a fast food restaurant with my friends last night and I think I ate too much and now I don't feel so good.
Rani: Well, what did you eat?
Dave: A cheeseburger and chips, a chicken burger, an apple pie.
Rani: Well, I'm not surprised!
Dave: Wait, I'm not finished, a chocolate muffin, an ice-cream and a coke.
Rani: Didn't you have any salad?
Dave: What – with all that?
Rani: Well, I'm not surprised you feel ill, Dave. You ate too much of all the wrong things! And this week's report is about health and fitness!
Dave: I really want to see this.

A. Focus on: Healthy food
Greg: And action!
Josh: You need to have a good diet to stay healthy and get energy every day. The food you put in your mouth goes into your stomach here, and through your body. We are what we eat! In a good canteen you can get a healthy lunch.
Maya: Would you like some nice fresh salad, Josh?
Josh: Mmm. Yes, please! You should eat a lot of fresh salad and vegetables, like this, every day.
Maya: And crisps? Smokey bacon? Salt 'n' vinegar? Ready salted? Cheese and onion?
Greg: Cheese and onion, … my favourite!
Maya: Not now, Greg!
Josh: No, thank you – no crisps today. You shouldn't eat a lot of salt. And not a lot of sugar. Well, some sugar is OK, for energy.
Maya: And lots of fruit. Lots and lots of fruit.
Josh: Yes, please. I'll have a banana.
Maya: Help yourself. And what would you like to drink? We've got fruit juices, still drinks, fizzy drinks.
Josh: Well, fruit juice and water are better than fizzy drinks in a can.

Maya: Josh!
Josh: Oh, sorry – pardon me! And remember: Drink lots of water! The human body needs at least two litres a day. Ahhh! Oh! So remember, you are what you eat.
Maya: What are you?
Greg: And cut! Great!
Maya: OK, Josh, Greg, are you ready to start the cooking scene now?
Josh/Greg: Yeah!
Maya: Good. Stand by, and action!
Josh: Now let's find out how to make a healthy and popular meal. And here's our star chef – Greg!
Greg: Hi, and welcome to the Action UK! kitchen! Today I'm cooking a curry. It's a spicy Indian dish.
Josh: It's hot!
Greg: Yes, curry powder is hot and spicy – and it's delicious! Did you know, curry is the most popular meal in Britain?
Josh: Is it really?
Greg: Yes! Curry is even more popular in Britain today than fish and chips! I'm making a vegetable curry, so I've got some potatoes and some spicy curry powder, some onions.
Josh: Garlic, I love garlic!
Greg: And some carrots, carrots, carrots? Where are the carrots, Maya?
Maya: I forgot to buy some carrots. Use something else.
Greg: I don't have any carrots, but I've got these. Some Indian ladies' fingers.
Josh: Some what?
Greg: These, ladies' fingers. Oh! Don't worry! They're not real ladies' fingers! It's just the name of this Indian vegetable! Have I got any rice, Josh?
Josh: Yes, here it is.
Greg: Thanks, Josh. And I'm going to need some salt. I want this to be a healthy dish so I'm not going to put too much salt in. First of all – let's chop the onions and garlic – here Josh, you can do the garlic!
Maya: Oh, come on. We're going to be here all day!
Greg: Ta daaa!
Josh: It looks great!
Greg: And because there's lots of vegetables in it, it's really good for you! And if you're not a vegetarian, you can make it with meat.
Josh: Mmm, that's a good curry. And now Maya can tell you the story of curry.
Maya: India was a British colony for a long time. Then, when the British left India in 1947, they brought curry back to Britain with them. Later many Indian people came to live in Britain. Some Indians opened curry restaurants called 'curry houses'. Soon the spicy food from India was very popular with everybody. Today you can find curry houses and Indian take-aways all over Britain. They've opened curry restaurants in the smallest villages. And you can always find curry on school dinner menues! Curry's so nice, it's not surprising that it has become Britain's favourite food!

Action UK! Studio
Rani: Ooh! I love a nice spicy curry! Mmmm, delicious! Oh sorry, Dave, all this food! Are you still not feeling very well?
Dave: Josh is right. I should be more careful about what I eat. And I think I need to get fitter again. I really should get more exercise.
Rani: Well, just have a look at Josh, Maya and Greg – and see who's the fittest!

B. That's Life: Fit – fitter – the fittest
Mum: I'm off to my Jazz Dance Class now – so I'll, er, see you later!
Greg: Bye, have fun!
Mum: Thanks. Bye, you two!
Josh/Maya: Bye!
Maya: I didn't know your mum went to jazz dance classes, Greg.
Greg: Yeah, well, she does. She thinks it's really good exercise, but I mean, jazz dance! That's not real exercise at all!
Maya: Hey, what do you mean? I do jazz dance, well, aerobics – and it really is hard work! Who knows, Greg, maybe your mum is fitter than you!
Greg: Fitter than me?! Oh come on, Maya!
Josh: You must be joking, Maya!
Greg: I mean, please! I play football! I'm much fitter than my mum, or you!
Josh: Maybe you're fitter than Maya but footballers aren't really the fittest people I know! I'm fit because I play badminton. People who play badminton are very fit, fitter than dancers and footballers!
Maya/Greg: You what?
Greg: Badminton? Badminton just looks cool, Josh, but it's not real exercise.
Josh: You have no idea!
Maya: Tell you what – let's see who's really the fittest, we could have a kind of competition.
Greg: What kind of competition?
Maya: A competition where we each have a go at football, badminton and aerobics.
Greg: So have you got all that?
Maya/Josh: Yeah ... yeah ... yeah.
Greg: Right then. On your marks ... get set ... GO! Another go anyone?
Josh: No! No way! Please no more!
Greg: Tired, Maya?
Maya: Yeah! – I – am! Footballers are fitter than I thought!
Josh: Hey, you two – badminton is a serious game. This is what you have to do. Er Maya, you have to hit it!
Maya: Oh, OK then.
Josh: OK – it's your turn – who wants to go first?
Greg: Ladies first, Maya!
Maya: No, Greg, please! After you!
Greg: No, it's alright.
Josh: OK. Are you ready?
Maya: Greg, your turn.
Josh: Come on, Greg.
Greg: I need a drink of water! I take it back, Josh! Badminton is more tiring than football!
Maya: I think you're right there, Greg! OK, boys. Come on then. Now let's see how fit you two really are!
Josh: Whatever, Maya!
Greg: Get on with it! Stop, Maya! I've had enough! I give in! My back hurts, my legs hurt, my feet hurt!
Josh: I need a rest.
Greg: Me, too!
Maya: Tired, boys?
Josh: You win. You win, badminton isn't as tiring as aerobics.
Greg: Yeah, Maya, you're the fittest, you must be to dance like that!

Action UK! Studio
Rani: We've got the three fittest reporters, Dave!
Dave: You're right there, Rani! I really must get fitter!
Rani: That's a great idea, Dave. Me, too! Well, that's all we've got time for. Tell everybody about next time, Dave. Dave? Dave! Oh well, see you next time. Bye! Dave?

Try it out!
Josh speaking to camera.
– You should eat lots of fresh salad

and vegetables, like this, every day.
Josh speaking to camera.
– You shouldn't eat a lot of salt.
Maya speaking to Greg.
– Footballers are fitter than I thought!
Greg speaking to Josh.
– Badminton is more tiring than football!
Greg speaking to Maya.
– You're the fittest …

Unit 6

Action UK! Studio
Rani: Hi! Here we are again.
Dave: Hello!
Rani: Today our reporters aren't in Greenwich.
Dave: That's right, Rani. They're at Broughton Castle!
Rani: Broughton Castle? Why Broughton?
Dave: Well, they often make films for TV and cinema at Broughton Castle – so our reporters decided to make their report there, too! And the owners still live in the castle!
Rani: Sounds interesting!
Dave: Yes! Well – we don't want to miss anything! Let's have a look!

A. Focus on: Broughton Castle

Josh's mum: I'm meeting Lord and Lady Saye at two.
Josh: OK.
Josh's mum: OK?
Greg: See you later.
Josh's mum: Bye!
Josh: OK. Are you ready, you two? Greg? Maya? Action!
Greg: Here we are, about 90 miles north west of London, at Broughton Castle. It's more than 700 years old.
Maya: And it's where they filmed 'Shakespeare in Love' and lots of other films and TV programmes.
Greg: We'll take you on a tour of the castle.
Maya: And maybe we'll meet Lord and Lady Saye! They're the owners and they live in the castle!
Greg: Let's go in.
Josh: Maya, you stand over there. You, too, Greg.
Maya: Here?
Josh: Great. Camera is rolling.
Maya: This is the Great Hall. And this is where they filmed 'Shakespeare in Love'.
Greg: Look at this armour.
Maya: Wow!
Greg: Oof – it's really heavy. Want to try, Maya?
Maya: Yeah, go on then.
Greg: Wow, look at these arms! Not real arms, silly! Here's a sword.
Maya: That looks really dangerous!
Greg: It is. Now let's go down to the castle dungeon. I bet they'll be really cold and dark and scary.
Maya: Er, no, they won't, Greg, Broughton Castle hasn't got any dungeons.
Greg: I thought all castles had dungeons.
Maya: No.
Josh: Cut. Great. So where are we going next?
Greg: The Tea Rooms.
Maya: Not yet, Greg. We've got more filming to do first.
Josh: Come on. OK, you two, are you ready?
Maya/Greg: Yep!
Josh: Maya! Action!
Greg: Here we are in the castle dining room. They made an advert for Kellogs Cornflakes in here! It was on TV!
Maya: That's right – the family still use the dining room – but not every day! They always have their Christmas dinner in here!
Greg: Mmm, Christmas dinner. I can almost smell the food. Roast turkey, roast potatoes, Christmas pudding. It's making me hungry! Can we go to the Tea Rooms now?
Josh: Cut! Greg, we're here to film the castle! First we'll go to the gardens. And then we'll go to the Tea Rooms.
Greg: OK.
Josh: Come on.
Maya: These are the castle gardens. Aren't they fantastic!
Greg: Yeah, cool. Trees, bushes, flowers, grass.
Maya: This is a walled garden.
Greg: Thanks, Maya. Now let's go to the Tea Rooms!
Josh: Er, wait.
Maya: Right, let's go to the Tea Rooms.
Josh: OK. It's OK now. Action!
Greg: Hi!
Maya: Thank you very much.
Waitress: You're welcome.
Greg: Thanks.
Maya: This is a traditional English cream tea: You drink tea with milk, of course!
Greg: And you eat these small cakes – called scones.
Maya: First you cut the scone in half, then you put strawberry jam on one half, and then thick clotted cream. Delicious!
Josh: Cut! Leave some for me! I want some, too!
Maya: I think Josh's mum is talking to Lord Saye! Here they come.
Mum: This is my son, Josh – and his friends.
J/M/G: Nice to meet you!
Lord Saye: Very nice having you here.
J/M/G: Thanks for letting us film here.
Greg: Great tea – and a great castle! I'd love to live in a castle!
Josh: Fantastic.
Greg: Would you like to go back and live in the past, Maya?
Maya: Hmm. No, I'd miss all my things.
Josh: Me, too!
Greg: Like what? What things would you miss?
Maya: Like my mobile, my CDs, my …

Action UK! Studio
Dave: Thanks for a great report, team! Would you like to go to Broughton Castle, Rani?
Rani: I'd love to! I love castles! And the gardens were lovely! What about you, Dave?
Dave: Well, castles are OK – but I prefer trips to places where you can do something!
Rani: Then you'll like our next film – Greg's dad took Greg, Maya and Josh to the seaside for the day.
Dave: Lucky things! What was it like?
Rani: Good … and not so good.
Dave: What d'you mean, Rani?
Rani: Well, see for yourself.

B. That's Life: A trip to the seaside

Dad: Well, here we are. The famous Southend Pier!
Maya: Wow!
Dad: I came here a lot when I was a boy.
Maya: Can we walk along it?
Dad: Sure. Come on, let's go.
Greg: How much further is it? Are we nearly there?
Josh: No! It's the longest pier in the world – it's almost two kilometres long!
Greg: Now you tell me! I'm hungry already. What are we walking for? There's a train!
Maya: Because it's more fun!
Josh: We'll get the train back, OK?

Dad:	Good idea, Josh. And this is as far as I go! Now: I'm going to have a nice day fishing. And catch lots of lovely fresh fish for tea! I'll be here until about … 5 o'clock – so I'll see you at the front of the pier at 5:30, OK? Here, Maya – you take the key, so you can get your things out of the car!
Maya:	Thanks! Good luck and have fun!
Josh:	See you later!
Greg:	Bye, Dad.
Maya:	OK boys! What's next?
Josh:	Let's look around Adventure Island – that looks cool!
Greg:	And then let's go to the beach! I want to go in the sea!
Maya:	Good idea! Let's go! Can I have four rocks, please?
Assistant:	11.96, please.
Maya:	Thanks.
Assistant:	Thank you. Here's your receipt.
Maya:	Thank you.
Assistant:	Thank you.
Maya:	I've got some real Southend Rock for my little sister. And here you are, boys! I got one for each of you, too!
Greg:	Thanks, Maya!
Josh:	What does this say?
Maya:	It says Southend Rock all the way through!
Greg:	Mmmmm – yum!
Josh:	It's really yummy!
Greg:	This is going to be really cool!
Maya:	I hope I don't feel ill!
Josh:	Don't worry, Maya! We'll look after you!
Greg:	Yes, you'll be fine with us!
Maya:	Yeah right, come on, let's go! That was really good!
Josh:	I wish there was something like this in Greenwich!
Maya:	Yeah, that would be great! What's next?
Greg:	Isn't it time to go to the beach now?
Josh:	We haven't been on that ride over there!
Maya:	Oh, come on, Josh, let's go to the beach now.
Josh:	Oh, OK then.
Greg:	Phew. Can we go in the water now?
Maya:	Sure!
Greg:	Come on, Josh. Or you'll be the last one in!
Josh:	Erm – you two go first – I think I'll take some photos! I don't think that's a very good idea.
Maya:	Yikes! The water's freeeeezing!
Josh:	Well, it is the North Sea! What did you expect?
Greg:	Come on – it's OK when you're in. Now I'm really hungry!
Maya:	You're not the only one!
Josh:	It's time to meet your dad! Let's hope he's caught a lot of fish!
Greg:	Hi, Dad!
Josh:	Hi! Did you have a good day?
Maya:	Show us the fish then! Let's have a look!
Dad:	Well. When I was a boy I always caught lots of fish. It's probably the wrong time of year for fishing! Or maybe I had the wrong bait or maybe today fish eat different food.
Greg:	Dad! What are you trying to say?
Maya:	I think he's trying to say he didn't catch any fish! Is that right?
Dad:	Yes, I'm afraid you're right, Maya!
Greg:	You mean you didn't catch a single fish – all day! I don't believe it! But we're really hungry!
Dad:	Well, I know where there's a really good fish and chip shop!
Greg:	Fish and chips? What are we waiting for? Let's go!

Action UK! Studio

Dave:	Well, that was a great day out at the seaside!
Rani:	Yeah, a walk along the pier, a fun park, playing on the beach, and fish and chips, mmmmm.
Dave:	Yes, d'you know, I think I'll have fish and chips tonight!
Rani:	Great idea! I think I will, too. Well, that's all we've got time for.
Dave:	See you next time!
Dave/Rani:	Bye!

Try it out!

Greg with others.
– We'll take you on a tour of the castle.
Dad speaking to reporters.
– I'll be here until about 5 o'clock.
Josh and Greg speaking to Maya.
– We'll look after you!
Yes, you'll be fine with us!

Unit 7

Action UK! Studio

Rani:	Hi, everybody!
Dave:	Hi! This is our last show for this year, Rani!
Rani:	Yeah. What's in today's show, Dave?
Dave:	Well! Today we're going to talk about visiting Britain. Maybe some things will surprise you!
Rani:	And maybe you already know a lot about Britain! Have a look.

A. Focus On: Typically British

Josh:	Special Report: Life in Britain. Take 1.
Maya:	Err. Who's doing the filming, Josh?
Josh:	Nobody! It's on remote.
Maya:	Oh, right! Sorry! Hi. Lots of people visit Britain. And maybe some day you will, too! So today we are making you a special video report.
Josh:	OK – change the picture now, Maya!
Greg:	Ah! Bacon and egg! My favourite.
Maya:	Greg … Greg … Greg!
Greg:	Oh! … er … maybe you think in Britain you'll have an English Breakfast every day! You know, bacon and egg and sausages and fried tomatoes every day. But – unfortunately – there isn't time in the morning!
Maya:	I usually just have cereal or toast with marmalade or jam. My family never has an English breakfast – but sometimes at the weekends we have croissants. Mmmmm! Tea, Greg?
Greg:	Please, Maya!
Maya:	Oh, there's no milk. We need some.
Josh:	In some parts of Britain the milkman still brings milk to your door very early in the morning. Here you go. And then he takes away the empty bottles.
Maya:	Thanks, Josh! Milk, Greg?
Greg:	Thanks, Maya!
Josh:	In Britain, people always queue. You know, wait in a line to go to the cinema.
Maya:	Or even to get into big sports events and to go to the toilet.
Josh:	Or for school dinners.
Maya:	Or even to just get on the bus. Sorry! After you! I think you were before me in the queue.
Greg:	Well, I was.
Josh:	You see, when everyone queues, it's much less stress!
Greg:	Oh no – I forgot the salt and vinegar. Mmmm. I love fish and chips with salt and vinegar!
Maya:	When you come to Britain,

75

	you can eat fish and chips, but there are lots of other kinds of take-away food, too. Like Chinese or pizza or Indian, American fast food and kebabs. I love kebabs!
Josh:	Me, too! Is that OK?
Maya:	Yeah, it's fine.
Josh:	OK, Greg!
Greg:	OK and action!
Josh:	Now it's time for cricket! It's a very British sport.
Maya:	How do you play cricket, Josh?
Josh:	Well, it's not easy. It's about hitting the ball with this and running between these – wickets!
Maya:	Right! I see!
Josh:	A game of cricket can go on for days and days.
Maya:	I'll never understand cricket. You love it or you hate it. I hate it!
Josh:	And I love it!
Greg:	OK and cut!
Maya:	What's next? Are you ready, Greg?
Greg:	OK! And … action!
Maya:	This is the Scottish flag. While you're up in bonnie Scotland, have a look at the Highland Games. That man has to throw that log as far as he can! It's called 'tossing the caber'! He's wearing a skirt: a traditional Scottish kilt. Come on, boys!
Greg:	Of course, Scottish boys and men don't wear kilts every day. They wear them for the Highland Games …
Josh:	… and for traditional Scottish dancing.
Maya:	No! Cut!
Josh:	Are you ready, Maya?
Maya:	Yeah! Helo pawb. Maya ydw i. Croesio i Cymru.
Greg:	Huh? What are you saying, Maya? We can't understand you!
Maya:	That's because I'm speaking Welsh. I went to Wales last year on holiday.
Josh:	Welsh? Well, what are you saying?
Maya:	I'm saying: Hello, everyone. My name's Maya! Welcome to Wales. Look, Croesio i Cymru. And that's the Welsh flag!
Greg:	It's got a dragon on it!
Josh:	You mean, they've got their own flag?
Maya:	Yeah, they do! Come on, boys! What are you two doing?
Josh:	We're Morris Dancers!
Greg:	And we're doing Morris Dancing! Look!
Maya:	Morris Dancing is really English! We haven't got many traditional dances. But this one is really famous. OK then, boys!
Greg:	OK, ready? Here are three last things for you!
Josh:	If you're coming to Britain, remember to change your money: We don't have euros. You need pounds.
Greg:	In Britain we drive on the left – so watch out when you cross the road!
Maya:	Also take one of these. You'll need it for your electrical things, like mobiles and CD players.
Josh:	Those were three important things! We hope you can remember everything!
Maya:	Well, that was the end of our last report for you.
Greg:	But it's not the end of the show, is it?
Josh:	No! Let's hand back to Dave and Rani in their studio!

Action UK! Studio

Rani:	And our reporters morris dancing!? Now I've seen it all!
Dave:	What a laugh! But that was a cool report about how we live in Britain.
Rani:	Yes. Do you like bacon and eggs for breakfast, Dave? It's our reporters!
Dave:	In the studio! Hi, you guys! Come and sit down!
Rani:	What a nice surprise! Tell us: What was it like to make your second Action UK! video?
Josh:	We had great fun!
Greg:	Yeah. Remember that girl at Broughton Castle?
Maya:	Oh, no!
Greg:	Look at this!
Josh:	I'm not sure about this shot but, Maya you stand there. Greg. No, I don't like that wall.
Maya:	Oh! You're so fussy, Josh!
Josh:	You have to be. I read that …
Tourist:	Are you making a film?
Maya:	Yes, we are.
Tourist:	Wow! Can I have your autograph!
Maya:	Sure.
Tourist:	Thanks! So where are you from … Hollywood?
Maya:	Huh? Er well, no, not Hollywood exactly. We're from Greenwich.
Tourist:	Oh, Right! Greenwich! So are you a famous star then?
Maya:	Well, not really famous.
Tourist:	When will your film be in the cinema?
Josh:	It won't – it's a film for schools.
Tourist:	Ohh, great!
Josh:	OK, not here. Come on.
Maya:	You two are so mean!
Dave:	Well, I'm sure everyone out there really enjoyed your reports! We did, that's for sure!
Rani:	And now it's time for the summer holidays for all of us!
Dave:	So, what are your plans for the summer, guys?
Greg:	I'm going to Scotland camping with my family. They've got some really cool castles with dungeons!
Rani:	What about you, Maya?
Maya:	I'm going to Spain.
Rani:	Sunny Spain! Ooh! That sounds fun.
Dave:	Are you going away, Josh?
Josh:	Yeah! We're flying to America! My mum's taking me to Hollywood!!
All:	Wow!
Rani:	Maybe you'll meet a famous Hollywood director!
Josh:	Maybe, you never know!
Rani:	Well, that's the end of Action UK! 2.
Dave:	So we'll see you next time!
All:	Bye!

Try it out!

Maya and Greg talking.
– Tea, Greg?
Please, Maya.
Maya and Greg talking.
– Milk, Greg?
Thanks, Maya.
Maya speaking to Greg.
– Oh, sorry. After you. I think you were before me in the queue.
Greg to himself.
– Mmmm …! I love fish and chips with salt and vinegar!